Steck-Vaughn

Reading Comprehension
Building Vocabulary and Meaning

Teacher's Guide

LEVEL

E

Reviewers

Roberta L. Frenkel

Director of English Language Arts
Community School District 3
New York, New York

Kim Winston-Radden

Fourth/Fifth Grade Teacher
MacDowell Elementary School
Detroit Public Schools
Detroit, Michigan

STECK-VAUGHN
A Harcourt Company

www.steck-vaughn.com

Contents

"Comprehension is the reason for reading."

(Armbruster, Lehr, & Osborn, 2001)

While this statement might seem obvious, it is the premise for *Steck-Vaughn Reading Comprehension: Building Vocabulary and Meaning*. Readers who understand what they read are good readers. Current research has identified what good readers do when they read. It has also shown that students can learn the strategies and processes of good readers—and that this improves their overall comprehension of text. *Steck-Vaughn Reading Comprehension: Building Vocabulary and Meaning* provides explicit instruction and practice in the strategies that good readers use.

"Comprehension is critically important to development of children's reading skills and therefore their ability to obtain an education."

(National Reading Panel, 2000)

To develop students' reading comprehension, *Steck-Vaughn Reading Comprehension: Building Vocabulary and Meaning* offers both a model of comprehension instruction and supportive context for instruction. Specifically, this series provides students with the following key elements:

- **Experience reading different genres.** Each student book includes a variety of fiction and nonfiction genres, such as folktales, historical fiction, science articles, and persuasive essays.

- **Opportunities for reading and rereading.** Each lesson includes a four-page reading selection that allows students to practice and apply skills, strategies, and knowledge. Specific tips in the Teacher's Guide offer help in promoting students' reading fluency.

- **Explicit instruction.** Each student lesson defines a focus comprehension skill and instructs students on how to use it. Tips placed at point-of-use provide suggestions that help students use the skill as they read.

- **Vocabulary and concept development through experience, reading, and discussion.** Each lesson taps into students' prior knowledge about the lesson's topic. Then the lesson develops their concept vocabulary through prereading discussion. Point-of-use placement of the vocabulary word definitions and a follow-up Vocabulary activity help students build and extend their vocabulary. Students can also use the Glossary to reference definitions and pronunciations of content vocabulary.

- **Teacher modeling use of the skill.** Students and teacher work through the skill as a group, using appropriate graphic organizers, which are provided on transparencies.

- **Meaningful discussion about text.** Students engage in thinking and discussion about the text on literal and higher, more inferential levels.

- **Guided practice followed by independent use of the comprehension skill.** Each lesson provides guided practice of the comprehension skill.

- **Experience writing different genres.** Each lesson gives students an opportunity to plan and write a personal response based on the genre of the selection, which reinforces connections between reading and writing.

- **Review of the comprehension skills.** Review pages after every six lessons help students maintain skills learned.

- **Standardized test practice.** Test formats that students will encounter on standardized tests are used on the Comprehension, Vocabulary, and Review pages.

Steck-Vaughn Reading Comprehension: Building Vocabulary and Meaning supports practices outlined in the National Reading Panel report, aligns with the International Reading Association (IRA) and National Council of Teachers of English (NCTE) Standards for the English Language Arts, and helps students achieve state and national literacy standards. The teaching framework of *Reading Comprehension: Building Vocabulary and Meaning* encompasses critical strategies for developing reading and writing skills.

Literacy Goals	Research Says:	*Reading Comprehension: Building Vocabulary and Meaning* Suggests:
Text Comprehension Comprehension allows students to read, understand, and critique text in a meaningful and productive way.	• "Comprehension instruction can effectively motivate and teach readers to learn and use comprehension strategies that benefit the reader." (National Reading Panel, 2000) • "Good comprehension instruction includes both explicit instruction in specific comprehension strategies and a great deal of time and opportunity for actual reading, writing, and discussion of text." (Duke & Pearson, 2002)	specific comprehension strategies that guide students to be aware of how well they are comprehending as they read and write.
Vocabulary Vocabulary knowledge is fundamental to reading comprehension as students cannot comprehend text without knowing what most of the words mean.	• "Vocabulary learning is effective when it entails active engagement in learning tasks." (National Reading Panel, 2000) • "To improve reading comprehension, children need rich, in-depth knowledge of words." (Nagy, 2000)	teaching strategies that include vocabulary instruction before, during, and after reading.
Fluency Fluency is the ability to read a text with speed and accuracy, which provides a bridge between word recognition and comprehension.	• "Frequent opportunities to practice identifying words through meaningful reading and writing experiences help the reader to achieve automatic word identification or automaticity." (Worthy & Broaddus, 2002)	opportunities for both oral reading and independent reading.
Writing Writing is an integral part of the comprehension process, as it is essential that students connect reading to writing.	• "Students should experience writing the range of genres we wish them to comprehend. Their instruction should emphasize connections between reading and writing." (Duke & Pearson, 2002)	independent prewriting with the use of graphic organizers and writing prompts that inspire a personal response.
Language Development Language development skills focus on students' communication skills by exploring and developing vocabulary.	• "Print exposes children to words outside their vocabulary far more effectively than conversational talk or other media like watching television." (Cunningham & Stanovich, 1998) • "Pairing books of fact and fiction allows students to become familiar with selected topics and vocabulary." (Camp, 2000)	print-rich environments in both fiction and nonfiction that provide opportunities and tools for developing language.

REFERENCES

Armbruster, B.B., Lehr, F., & Osborn, J. (2001). *Put reading first: The research building blocks for teaching children to read.* Washington, DC: National Institute for Literacy.

Camp, D. (2000). It takes two: Teaching with twin texts of fact and fiction. *The Reading Teacher, 53*(5) 400–408.

Cunningham, A.E., & Stanovich, K. (1998). What reading does for the mind. *American Educator, 22,* 8–15.

Duke, N.K., & Pearson, D. (2002). Effective practices for developing reading comprehension. Farstrup, A.E., & Samuels, S.J. (Eds.) *What research has to say about reading instruction* (4th ed., pp. 205–242). Newark, DE: International Reading Association.

Nagy, W.E. (2000). *Teaching vocabulary to improve reading comprehension.* Urbana, IL: National Council of Teachers of English and Newark, DE: International Reading Association. (ERIC Document Reproduction No. ED298471)

National Reading Panel. (2000). *Teaching children to read: An evidence-based assessment of the scientific research literature on reading and its implications for reading instruction. Reports of the subgroups.* Bethesda, MD: Author. (ERIC Document Reproduction No. ED444127)

Teal, W.H., & Shanahan, T. (2001). Ignoring the essential: Myths about fluency. *Illinois Reading Council Journal, 29*(3), 5–8.

Worthy, J., & Broaddus, K. (2002). Fluency beyond the primary grades: From group performance to silent, independent reading. *The Reading Teacher, 55*(4), 334–344.

Student Editions

Each Student Edition consists of twelve lessons and eight review pages. Each lesson begins with a four-page reading selection that is followed by four pages of comprehension, vocabulary, focus skill, and writing practice.

The reading selections include high-interest fiction and nonfiction written in a variety of literary genres, such as science articles, folktales, biographies, historical fiction, and others. Colorful photographs, inviting illustrations, and vibrant lesson openers support the text, aid in comprehension, and engage the reader.

The selections have visual supports appropriate to the content and skill, such as maps, timelines, charts, and diagrams. These visuals enhance the text and give students experience with a variety of informational formats.

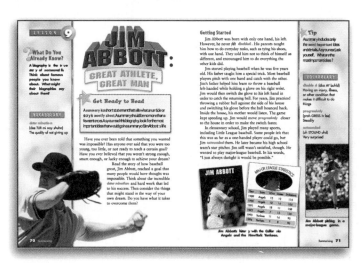

Following each selection, students use a graphic organizer designed to teach the comprehension focus skill and provide a model for independent writing. Students then use the same or a similar graphic organizer to prewrite for an original story or article. The progression through the lesson helps students connect reading to writing.

Teacher's Guides

The Teacher's Guide includes a plan for each lesson. The easy-to-use lesson plans provide explicit reading comprehension and vocabulary instruction, as well as opportunities to extend the activities for individual needs.

Each lesson plan begins with a list of standards covered in the lesson for reading, vocabulary, writing, and, for nonfiction selections, the content area. Next, an oral language warm-up builds on background knowledge and is followed by an activity that introduces the vocabulary words. Each lesson plan has a model Graphic Organizer transparency that teachers can use to introduce the comprehension focus skill and set the purpose for reading.

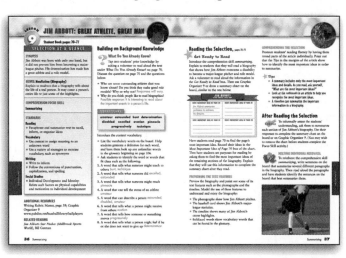

All lessons provide both formal and informal assessment opportunities. Each independent writing activity has a 4-point scoring rubric and a student writing rubric master to encourage student self-assessment.

Skills and Standards Chart

Title	Genre	Comprehension Focus Skill	Reading Standards	Vocabulary and Writing Standards	Content Standards
Lesson 1 *The Wonders of Caves*	Nonfiction/ Science Article	Identifying Main Idea/ Supporting Details	• Determine a text's main ideas and how those ideas are supported with details. • Use organizational features of texts such as glossaries and subheadings	**Vocabulary** • Use context to assign meaning to words • Locate meanings, pronunciations, and spellings using dictionaries and glossaries **Writing** • Write to inform	**Science** Earth Science: Properties of Earth materials
Lesson 2 *Dinner Disaster!*	Fiction/ Humorous Story	Analyzing Characters	• Analyze characters, including their feelings, traits, motivations, relationships, and changes they undergo	**Vocabulary** • Use context to assign meaning to words • Determine meanings of derivatives by applying knowledge of the meanings of root words and affixes **Writing** • Write to narrate • Follow the conventions of punctuation, capitalization, and spelling	
Lesson 3 *The Coldest Race on Earth: Alaska's Iditarod*	Nonfiction/ Social Studies Article	Sequencing	• Analyze text that is organized in sequential or chronological order • Use organizational and graphic features of texts such as glossaries or maps	**Vocabulary** • Know the literal meaning of words • Extend awareness of analogies **Writing** • Write to explain • Follow the conventions of punctuation, capitalization, and spelling	**Social Studies** People, Places, and Environments: Describe ways that historical events have been influenced by physical and human geographic factors in regional settings
Lesson 4 *Time for Travel!*	Fiction/ Science Fiction	Making Predictions	• Make and revise predictions • Understand and distinguish literary forms such as science fiction	**Vocabulary** • Know the literal meaning of words • Use context to assign meaning to words **Writing** • Write to explain • Follow the conventions of punctuation, capitalization, and spelling	
Lesson 5 *Creatures of the Deep*	Nonfiction/ Science Article	Comparing and Contrasting	• Connect, compare, and contrast ideas, themes, and issues • Use organizational features of texts such as glossaries and subheadings	**Vocabulary** • Use context to assign meaning to words • Extend awareness of similes **Writing** • Write to inform and describe • Follow the conventions of punctuation, capitalization, and spelling	**Science** Life Science: Characteristics of organisms; Organisms and environments
Lesson 6 *The Greatest Trip Ever*	Fiction/ Realistic Story	Making Inferences	• Draw inferences such as conclusions or generalizations and support them with text evidence and experience	**Vocabulary** • Know the literal meaning of words • Use context to assign meaning to words **Writing** • Create multiple-paragraph narrative compositions including developing a situation or plot, setting, and ending	

Title	Genre	Comprehension Focus Skill	Reading Standards	Vocabulary and Writing Standards	Content Standards
Lesson 7 *Welcome to Hawaii!*	Nonfiction/ Social Studies Article	Distinguishing Fact from Opinion	• Distinguish facts and opinions in texts	**Vocabulary** • Use a variety of strategies to determine meaning and increase vocabulary such as synonyms and word relationships • Use root words and affixes to analyze the meaning of complex words **Writing** • Write and expository description • Follow the conventions of punctuation, capitalization, and spelling	**Social Studies** People, Places and Environments: Locate and distinguish among varying landforms and geographic features
Lesson 8 *The Dancing Bear*	Fiction/ Realistic Story	Identifying Plot	• Recognize and analyze story plot, setting, and problem resolution • Analyze characters, including their motivations and conflicts	**Vocabulary** • Know the literal meaning of words • Draw on experiences to bring meanings to words in context such as interpreting multiple-meaning words **Writing** • Create multiple-paragraph narrative compositions including developing a situation or plot, setting, and ending	
Lesson 9 *Jim Abbott: Great Athlete, Great Man*	Nonfiction/ Biography	Summarizing	• Paraphrase and summarize text to recall, inform, or organize ideas	**Vocabulary** • Use assign meaning to an unknown word • Use a variety of strategies to increase vocabulary, such as synonyms **Writing** • Write to inform • Follow the conventions of punctuation, capitalization, and spelling	**Social Studies** Individual Development and Identity: Relate such factors as physical capabilities and motivation to individual development
Lesson 10 *Waves of Terror*	Nonfiction/ Science Article	Identifying Cause and Effect	• Identify cause and effect • Use the text's structure or progression of ideas such as cause and effect or chronology to locate and recall information	**Vocabulary** • Know the literal meaning of words • Understand and explain frequently used synonyms **Writing** • Write to explain • Follow the conventions of punctuation, capitalization, and spelling	**Science** Earth and Space Science: Changes in Earth and sky
Lesson 11 *Searching for Bigfoot*	Fiction/ Narrative Story	Making Judgments	• Offer observations, make connections, react, speculate, interpret, and raise questions in response to texts • Draw inferences such as conclusions or generalizations and support them with text evidence and experience	**Vocabulary** • Use context to assign meaning to unknown words • Extend awareness of analogies and idiomatic language previously learned **Writing** • Use information and ideas from other subject areas and personal experiences to form and express opinions and judgements	
Lesson 12 *Look Out! The World's Most Dangerous Animals*	Nonfiction/ Science Article	Recognizing Author's Purpose	• Identify the purposes of different types of texts such as to inform, influence, express, or entertain • Describe author's purpose and perspective and how it influences the text and how authors organize information in specific ways	**Vocabulary** • Know the literal meaning of words • Use word origins to determine the meaning of unknown words **Writing** • Establish a purpose for writing • Write to inform, persuade, or entertain	**Science** Life Science: Characteristics of organisms; Organisms and environments

Colorful photographs and attractive illustrations create **engaging lesson openers** that support the fiction and nonfiction texts, aid in comprehension, and engage the reader.

Maps and other **visual supports** appear in each lesson to enhance the text and students' comprehension.

What Do You Already Know? taps into students' prior knowledge and develops oral language.

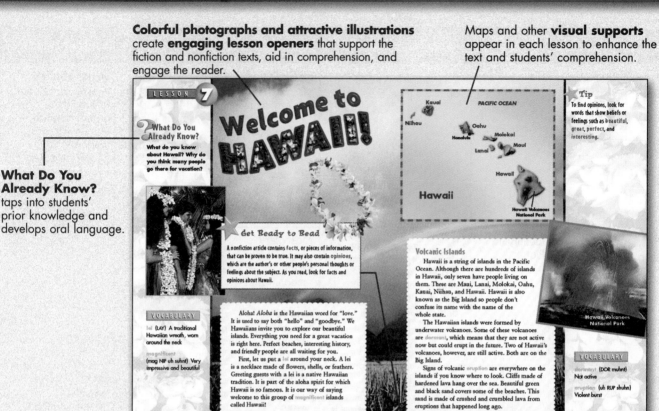

Get Ready to Read introduces the comprehension focus skill and helps students set a purpose for reading.

Comprehension Tips support reading and help students apply the comprehension skill as they read. Key words "pop" in bold, red type.

Vocabulary words are highlighted in the text and defined, with pronunciation, at point of use. Each vocabulary word also appears in the Glossary.

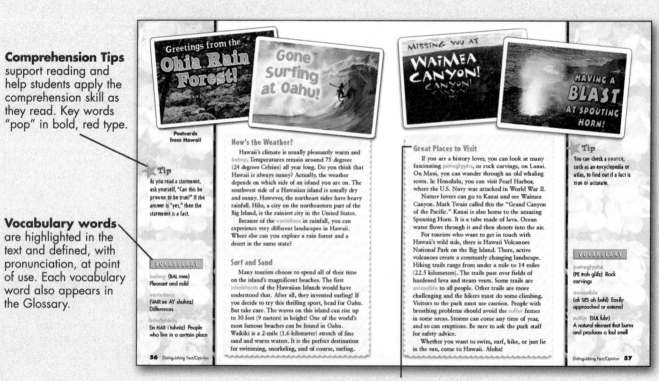

Subheads help students comprehend the structure of the text by "chunking."

Comprehension Check provides opportunities to demonstrate comprehension of text on literal and higher, more inferential levels.
Test Preparation formats, which may also appear on the *Vocabulary Builder* page, equip students for success on standardized tests.

Vocabulary Builder provides strategies for confirming meaning and language development.

Extend Your Vocabulary provides engaging activities and lessons that enhance vocabulary with more challenging concepts.

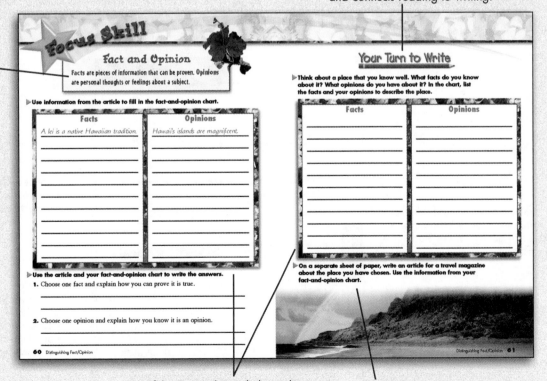

Comprehension Check

▶ **Fill in the circle next to the best answer.**

1. Which of the following best describes who this article was written for?

Ⓐ People currently living in Hawaii
Ⓑ People who used to live in Hawaii but moved away
Ⓒ People who have visited Hawaii many times before
Ⓓ People who have never visited Hawaii before

2. Which sentence from the article best helps you visualize Hawaii?

Ⓔ Everything you need for a great vacation is right here.
Ⓕ Visitors to the park must use caution.
Ⓖ Cliffs made of hardened lava hang over the sea.
Ⓗ After all, they invented surfing!

3. Why should you be careful on the beaches of Oahu?

Ⓐ There are active volcanoes.
Ⓑ The cliffs are very tall.
Ⓒ The people there are unfriendly.
Ⓓ The waves get very high.

4. Where would you stay in Hawaii if you wanted sunny weather?

Ⓔ The northeastern part of the Big Island
Ⓕ The northwest side of an island
Ⓖ The southwest side of an island
Ⓗ The city of Hilo

▶ **Answer the questions below in complete sentences.**

5. How do you think the author feels about Hawaii? Tell why.

_____
_____
_____

6. Which part of Hawaii would you most like to visit? Tell why.

_____
_____
_____

58 Distinguishing Fact/Opinion

Vocabulary Builder

▶ **Write the word from the box that best fits with each group of words.**

| balmy | dormant | inhabitants | lei |
| magnificent | petroglyphs | sulfur | variations |

1. cave paintings, rock carvings, _____
2. necklace, wreath, _____
3. differences, variety, _____
4. gas, fumes, _____
5. impressive, awesome, _____
6. pleasant, warm, _____
7. inactive, at rest, _____
8. natives, locals, _____

EXTEND YOUR VOCABULARY

Suffixes A suffix is a word part that is added to the end of a word to change its meaning.

| -tion = the act or state of | -ible = able to be |

▶ **Find each word with a suffix. Underline the root word and circle the suffix. Then write the definition on the line.**

9. Some volcanoes are accessible to tourists of all ages.

10. One volcano is off limits due to a recent eruption.

Distinguishing Fact/Opinion **59**

Focus Skill instructional box **reviews** the comprehension focus skill for each lesson.

Your Turn to Write emphasizes major writing forms, purposes, and processes and connects reading to writing.

Focus Skill

Fact and Opinion

Facts are pieces of information that can be proven. Opinions are personal thoughts or feelings about a subject.

▶ **Use information from the article to fill in the fact-and-opinion chart.**

Facts	Opinions
A lei is a native Hawaiian tradition.	Hawaii's islands are magnificent.

▶ **Use the article and your fact-and-opinion chart to write the answers.**

1. Choose one fact and explain how you can prove it is true.

_____
_____

2. Choose one opinion and explain how you know it is an opinion.

_____
_____

60 Distinguishing Fact/Opinion

Your Turn to Write

▶ **Think about a place that you know well. What facts do you know about it? What opinions do you have about it? In the chart, list the facts and your opinions to describe the place.**

Facts	Opinions

▶ **On a separate sheet of paper, write an article for a travel magazine about the place you have chosen. Use the information from your fact-and-opinion chart.**

Distinguishing Fact/Opinion **61**

Graphic Organizers help students apply the comprehension focus skill and provide a model for independent writing.

A **Writing** prompt suggests ideas for independent writing in a variety of formats.

Sample Teacher's Guide Lesson

Building on Background Knowledge taps into students' prior knowledge and provides questions that promote discussion.

Get Ready to Read introduces the comprehension focus skill for each lesson, including a graphic organizer on a **Transparency** found at the back of this guide.

Comprehending the Selection checks comprehension, helps students improve fluency, and provides easy reference to the comprehension tips.

Assessment aids teachers in checking students' comprehension after each reading selection.

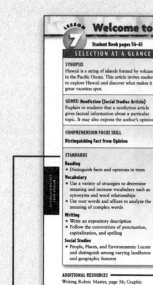

Clear **Standards** list benchmarks for reading, vocabulary, writing, and content areas.

Additional Resources are provided to enhance and extend each lesson.

Vocabulary provides ways to introduce each lesson's vocabulary words through engaging exercises.

Previewing the Text Features highlights the specific features and visual supports.

Meeting Individual Needs/ESL provides extended learning for different learner groups, including ESL students.

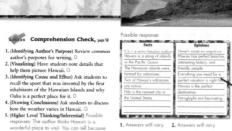

Answers and additional questions are provided for each activity in the Student Edition.

Reduced **Graphic Organizer** helps assess students' performance on the *Focus Skill* page.

A 4-point **Scoring Rubric** provides teachers with a means to assess students' performance on each type of independent writing. For each lesson, a Writing Rubric Master for students based on this rubric is also provided.

Series Scope and Sequence

Reading Skills	Level A	Level B	Level C	Level D	Level E	Level F
COMPREHENSION						
Literal Comprehension						
Understanding Facts and Details	•	•	•	•	•	•
Identifying Plot	•	•	•	•	•	•
Identifying Main Idea and Supporting Details	•	•	•	•	•	•
Summarizing		•	•	•		•
Identifying Text Structure						•
Interpretive Skills						
Retelling	•					
Distinguishing Fact from Opinion		•	•	•	•	
Sequencing	•	•	•	•	•	
Identifying Cause and Effect	•	•	•	•	•	
Recognizing Setting	•	•	•	•	•	
Comparing and Contrasting	•	•	•	•	•	•
Critical Thinking						
Categorizing and Classifying	•	•				
Creative Response	•	•				
Understanding Realism and Fantasy	•	•				
Making Predictions	•	•	•	•	•	•
Drawing Conclusions		•	•	•	•	•
Identifying Author's Purpose		•	•	•	•	•
Analyzing Character			•	•	•	•
Making Inferences				•	•	•
Making Judgments					•	
Identifying Theme						•
VOCABULARY						
Naming Words	•	•				
Rhyming Words		•				
Classifying		•				
Context Clues	•	•	•	•	•	•
Synonyms	•	•	•	•	•	•
Antonyms			•	•	•	•
Words with Multiple Meanings			•	•	•	
Dictionary Skills			•	•	•	•
Prefixes			•	•	•	•
Suffixes			•	•	•	•
Compound Words			•	•	•	
Root Words			•	•	•	•
Analogies				•	•	•
Similes					•	•
Greek and Latin Roots					•	•

THE WONDERS OF CAVES

Student Book pages 2–9

SELECTION AT A GLANCE

SYNOPSIS
This article explains how spelunking—the hobby of exploring caves—can reveal many natural wonders, both living and nonliving.

GENRE: Nonfiction (Science Article)
Explain to students that a nonfiction article provides factual information on a topic.

COMPREHENSION FOCUS SKILL
Identifying Main Idea/Supporting Details

STANDARDS

Reading
- Determine a text's main ideas and how those ideas are supported with details
- Use organizational features of texts such as glossaries and subheadings

Vocabulary
- Use context to assign meaning to words
- Locate meanings, pronunciations, and spellings using dictionaries and glossaries

Writing
- Write to inform

Science
- Earth Science: Properties of Earth materials

ADDITIONAL RESOURCES
Writing Rubric Master, page 50; Graphic Organizer 1
www.goodearthgraphics.com/showcave.html

RELATED READING
Caves (The Wonders of Our World), Neil Morris

Building on Background Knowledge

? What Do You Already Know?
Tap into students' prior knowledge by asking a volunteer to read aloud the text under *What Do You Already Know?* on page 2. Have students discuss the questions on page 2 and the questions below.

- What might the inside of a cave be like? Possible responses: dark, damp, cool
- How do you think caves are formed? Possible response: Water erodes rocks underground.
- What tools might you need to explore a cave? Possible responses: flashlights, ropes

VOCABULARY

**chambers   descent   enthusiastic   fragile
reliable   spectacular   spelunking
stalactites   stalagmites   unique**

Introduce the content vocabulary by using the following "Word Origin" technique.

- Write the vocabulary words on the board and help students make up a definition for each. Have them look up any unfamiliar words in the glossary beginning on page 106.
- Explain to students that many words in our language come from other languages. Draw a chart similar to the one below. Have students complete the chart with vocabulary words.

Foreign Word	Origin	Meaning	English Word
stalagm/stalakt	Greek	to drip	stalagmites, stalactites
unicus	Latin	one	unique
chambre	French	room	chambers
spelunx	Greek	cave	spelunking
enthousiastikos	Greek	inspired	enthusiastic
fragilis	Latin	to break	fragile
descendre	Old French	to go down	descent
relier	Old French	to bind	reliable
spectare	Latin	to look at	spectacular

Reading the Selection, pages 2-5

⭐ Get Ready to Read

Introduce the comprehension skill *identifying main idea/supporting details*. Explain to students that they will read an article that includes main ideas and details about exploring caves. Ask a volunteer to read the information in the *Get Ready to Read* box. Then use Graphic Organizer 1 or draw a main idea/supporting details chart on the board, similar to the one below.

MAIN IDEA
Spelunking is the hobby of exploring caves.

SUPPORTING DETAIL	SUPPORTING DETAIL	SUPPORTING DETAIL
You may see amazing rocks.		

Have students read the first page to find the main idea of the article. Record their responses in the top section of the chart. Then ask them to reread the last six sentences on the first page to find one detail that supports this main idea. Record the detail in the chart. Then have students set purposes for reading by asking them to look for other supporting details as they read. Explain that they will use these examples to complete the main idea/supporting details chart later.

PREVIEWING THE TEXT FEATURES

Preview the article with students. Point out one or more text features such as the photographs, diagrams, and subheads. Model how to use these features to understand and appreciate the article:

- The photographs show what a cave may look like and some creatures that live there.
- A diagram shows knots that people tie on their ropes when they explore caves.
- The subheads show what each section is about.
- Boldfaced words show vocabulary words that can be found in the glossary.

COMPREHENDING THE SELECTION

To promote students' fluency, tape record a fluent reading of the article and have students read along with the recording. Point out that the *Tips* in the margins of the article help students identify main ideas and supporting details as they read.

⭐ Tips

- A **subhead** can tell you the main idea of a section.
- To find supporting details, look for **facts** or **examples** that give more information about the main idea.
- Paragraphs also have a main idea. Phrases such as "**for example**" can help you find supporting details.

After Reading the Selection

ASSESS To informally assess students' understanding, ask them to tell the main idea of the article. Then ask them to tell the details that support the main idea. Use their responses to complete the main idea/supporting details chart on Graphic Organizer 1 or on the board. (You may wish to remove the chart before students complete the Focus Skill activity.)

MEETING INDIVIDUAL NEEDS/ESL

Have students work with partners to create picture dictionary entries with labels and illustrations of key terms and concepts from the article.

ASSESS **Comprehension Check,** page 6

1. (**Recalling Details**) Tell students to skim the text on page 4 to find what spelunkers need. C
2. (**Recognizing Author's Purpose**) Review common author's purposes for writing. F
3. (**Identifying Cause and Effect**) Ask students to reread the section about how caves form. A
4. (**Making Inferences**) Ask students which answer is supported by details in the article. H
5. (**Higher Level Thinking/Inferential**) Possible response: If the knot came undone, the spelunker could fall or get hurt.
6. (**Higher Level Thinking/Inferential**) Possible response: They must be able to live in cold, dark conditions.

 ASSESS **Vocabulary Builder,** page 7

Have students recall the word origin chart they completed before reading, and ask them to give the meaning of each vocabulary word in their own words. Then have students complete page 7 independently.

Answers for Vocabulary Builder: 1. large rooms **2.** downward climb **3.** one of a kind **4.** amazing **5.** excited **6.** dependable **7.** easily broken
Extend Your Vocabulary: 8. stalactites; pieces of rock that hang from the roof of a cave **9.** spelunking; the hobby of exploring caves **10.** stalagmites; pieces of rock that stick up from the floor of a cave

 **Focus Skill**

Main Idea and Supporting Details, page 8
Ask a volunteer to read aloud the information in the instructional box. Recall with students the chart they used earlier to record the main idea and supporting details. Then have them complete the page on their own, referring to the article as needed.

Possible response:

MAIN IDEA		
Spelunking allows people to see the many wonders of caves.		
SUPPORTING DETAIL	**SUPPORTING DETAIL**	**SUPPORTING DETAIL**
You may see amazing rocks.	You may see bubbling streams and huge lakes.	You can see unusual animals.

1. Answers will vary. Possible response: Page 4, paragraph 2: Spelunking equipment is similar to mountain climbing equipment.
2. Possible response: Spelunkers use strong ropes. Spelunkers use special tools to attach to cave walls.

Your Turn to Write, page 9
Explain to students that a main idea/supporting details chart will help them write an article about an outdoor activity they enjoy. Remind them to include details that tell about any special training or equipment they need and what they can see or learn by taking part in the activity.

SCORING RUBRIC

Nonfiction Article About an Activity
Distribute copies of the Writing Rubric Master on page 50 to students before they write.

SCORE 4 The article tells about an outdoor activity. It has a clear main idea and includes three or more supporting details. There are no errors in grammar, usage, and mechanics.

SCORE 3 The article tells about an outdoor activity. It has a main idea and includes two supporting details. There are a few errors in grammar, usage, and mechanics.

SCORE 2 The article tells about an outdoor activity. It has a main idea and includes just one supporting detail. There are several errors in grammar, usage, and mechanics.

SCORE 1 The article is incomplete. It does not tell about an outdoor activity, or is lacking supporting details. There are numerous errors in grammar, usage, and mechanics.

Dinner Disaster!

Student Book pages 10–17

SELECTION AT A GLANCE

SYNOPSIS
Alita decides that she and her brother, Paul, will surprise Mom by making dinner. Although Alita chooses a simple recipe, things don't turn out quite as she planned.

GENRE: Fiction (Humorous Story)
Explain to students that fiction usually has well-developed characters that talk and act like real people. It also has a plot with a beginning, middle, and end.

COMPREHENSION FOCUS SKILL
Analyzing Characters

STANDARDS
Reading
- Analyze characters, including their feelings, traits, motivations, relationships, and the changes in their lives

Vocabulary
- Use context to assign meaning to words
- Determine meanings of derivatives by applying knowledge of the meanings of root words and affixes

Writing
- Write narratives using first person
- Follow the conventions of punctuation, capitalization, and spelling

ADDITIONAL RESOURCES
Writing Rubric Master, page 51; Graphic Organizer 2
www.kidsdomain.org/holiday/cinco/recipes.html

RELATED READING
Kids Around the World Cook!: The Best Foods and Recipes from Many Lands, Arlette N. Braman

Building on Background Knowledge

What Do You Already Know?
Ask volunteers to recall characters they especially liked in other fictional stories. Then ask a volunteer to read aloud the text under *What Do You Already Know?* on page 10. Have students discuss the questions on page 10 and the questions below.

- Have you ever used a recipe? Did the meal turn out the way you planned? Answers will vary.
- What are some things you've tried to do to help that didn't turn out quite as you expected? Answers will vary.

VOCABULARY

affectionately	anxious	cantaloupe
complicate	doubtful	expression
generous	ingredients	nudging	spewed

Introduce the content vocabulary by using the following "Questioning" technique.

- Write the vocabulary words on the board. Help students make up a definition for each word, and suggest that they look up any unfamiliar words in the glossary beginning on page 106.
- Ask the following questions to promote discussion of the vocabulary words.
1. What does a cantaloupe look and taste like?
2. What are some ingredients that might go in a fruit salad?
3. Do you like having someone nudging you?
4. What is a doubtful expression?
5. Would you be anxious if food spewed out of a blender?
6. If someone helps you with your homework, does that complicate things or make things easier?
7. Do dogs and cats both act affectionately?
8. Would you rather have a generous helping of spinach or a small one?

Reading the Selection, pages 10–13

Get Ready to Read

Introduce the comprehension skill *analyzing characters*. Explain to students that they will read a humorous story about a character who tries to do something but doesn't quite succeed. Ask a volunteer to read the information in the *Get Ready to Read* box. Then use Graphic Organizer 2 or draw a character chart on the board, similar to the one below.

What Alita Is Like	Story Clues
Alita likes to try new things.	She wants to make dinner.
What Paul Is Like	**Story Clues**

Have students read the first page of the story to find out what Alita is like. Explain that a character's actions are one way readers can learn what the character is like. Record students' responses in the top sections of the chart. Then have students set purposes for reading by asking them to look for other examples of words, thoughts, and actions that show what Alita is like. Explain that they will use these examples to complete the character chart later.

PREVIEWING THE TEXT FEATURES

Preview the story with students. Point out text features such as the recipe card and dialogue. Model how to use these features to appreciate the story:

- Words in quotation marks show the exact words spoken by Alita, Paul, and Mom and give clues about what they are like.
- The recipe card shows the ingredients and instructions to make quesadillas.
- Illustrations give readers details about the characters that may not be included in the text.
- Boldfaced words show vocabulary words that can be found in the glossary.

COMPREHENDING THE SELECTION

To promote students' fluency, have them read aloud in small groups. Different students can read dialogue for the three characters and one student can read the narrative sections. Point out that the *Tips* in the margins of the story help readers understand the characters as they read.

Tips

- What other characters **say** and **feel** can give you clues about the main character. What does Mom's reaction tell you about Alita?
- Pay attention to what Alita and Paul **say**, **think**, and **do**. What kind of people do you think they are?
- Think about what Paul does and what Alita does. How do their **actions** show that they are different?

After Reading the Selection

ASSESS To informally assess students' understanding, ask them to name some different ways that readers can learn what characters are like. Then have them describe Alita and Paul to complete the character chart on Graphic Organizer 2 or on the board. (You may wish to remove the chart before students complete the Focus Skill activity.)

MEETING INDIVIDUAL NEEDS/ESL

Have students work in groups of three. Have them role-play parts of the story. Encourage them to use story vocabulary and other words and phrases in their role-plays.

 Comprehension Check, page 14

1. (**Identifying Main Idea**) Tell students that the main idea of a story includes general information, but not details. The story is about twins who try to make dinner for their mother.

2. (**Recalling Details**) Ask students to find what Alita said to her brother after she nudged him. Alita's mother is starting a new job, and Alita thinks she will be too tired to cook at the end of her first day.

3. (**Making Predictions**) Remind students to use clues from the story and what they know from real life to make a prediction. Possible response: You can predict that Alita will make a mess when she tries to cook dinner.

4. (**Identifying Plot**) Ask students what ingredient Paul and Alita cannot find at the market. Alita and Paul can't find cilantro, so they decide to buy cinnamon instead.

5. (**Sequencing**) The first step is grating the cheese.

6. (**Higher Level Thinking/Inferential**) Mom is proud of Alita's efforts even though Alita made a mistake.

 Vocabulary Builder, page 15

Have students tell the meaning of each vocabulary word in their own words. Then have them complete page 15 independently.

Answers for Vocabulary Builder: 1. D **2.** G **3.** A **4.** F **5.** C **6.** H **7.** B **8.** G
Extend Your Vocabulary: 9. doubtful; full of uncertainty **10.** affectionately; in a loving way

Character, page 16
Ask a volunteer to read aloud the information in the instructional box. Recall with students the chart they began earlier to make notes about characters. Then have them complete the page on their own, referring back to the story as needed.

Possible response:

What Alita Is Like	Story Clues
Alita is careless.	She used cinnamon instead of cilantro on the quesadillas.

What Paul Is Like	Story Clues
Paul is careful.	He tells Alita not to use the blender.

1. Possible response: Alita does not think before she does things, while Paul is cautious.
2. Answers will vary.

 Your Turn to Write, page 17
Explain to students that a character chart will help them write a story about a sticky situation they got into with another person. Remind them to include details telling what they and the other person said, did, and thought.

SCORING RUBRIC

Story About a Sticky Situation
Distribute copies of the Writing Rubric Master on page 51 to students before they write.

SCORE 4 The story tells about a sticky situation and is written in first person. It develops the characters by telling what they said, did, and thought. There are few or no errors in grammar, usage, and mechanics.

SCORE 3 The story tells about a sticky situation and is written in first person. It includes some details about what the characters said, did, or thought. There are a few errors in grammar, usage, and mechanics.

SCORE 2 The story tells about a sticky situation, but is not written in first person. It has few details about what the characters said, did, or thought. There are several errors in grammar, usage, and mechanics.

SCORE 1 The story is incomplete. It does not tell about a sticky situation, or is lacking details to develop the characters. There are numerous errors in grammar, usage, and mechanics.

SEQUENCING

SELECTION AT A GLANCE

SYNOPSIS
This article describes the Iditarod Sled Dog Race, a grueling journey over 1100 miles of frozen rivers and snowy Alaskan tundra.

GENRE: Nonfiction (Social Studies Article)
Tell students that a social studies article provides factual information on a topic related to a place or the way people live in some part of the earth.

COMPREHENSION FOCUS SKILL
Sequencing

STANDARDS
Reading
- Analyze text that is organized in sequential or chronological order
- Use organizational and graphic features of texts such as glossaries and maps

Vocabulary
- Understand the literal meaning of words
- Extend awareness of analogies

Writing
- Write to explain
- Follow the conventions of punctuation, capitalization, and spelling

Social Studies
- People, Places, and Environments: Describe the ways that historical events have been influenced by physical and human geographic factors in regional settings

ADDITIONAL RESOURCES
Writing Rubric Master, page 52; Graphic Organizer 3
www2.grand-forks.k12.nd.us/iditarod/iditarod.html

RELATED READING
Storm Run: The Story of the First Woman to Win the Iditarod Sled Dog Race, Libby Riddles

Building on Background Knowledge

? What Do You Already Know?
Tap into students' prior knowledge about Alaska and sled dogs by asking a volunteer to read aloud the text under *What Do You Already Know?* on page 18. Have students discuss the questions that are on page 18 and the questions below.

- What do you think winters are like in Alaska? Possible response: dark, very cold, and snowy
- Would it be easy for people to drive from place to place? If not, how do you suppose they travel long distances in winter? Possible responses: The weather might make travel difficult. People might travel by plane or dog sled.
- What do you think it would be like to be a part of a long dog sled race in Alaska? Possible response: It might be very lonely, fun, or cold.

VOCABULARY

effective era massive muscular obstacle
participate remembrance territory tundra vital

Introduce the content vocabulary.

- Write the vocabulary words on the board and have students make up a definition for each one. Have them look up any unfamiliar words in the glossary beginning on page 106.
- On the board prepare a chart with three columns, one each for nouns, adjectives, and verbs.
- Have volunteers write the vocabulary words in the correct columns on the chart. Then have each student use one of the words in a sentence.

Reading the Selection, pages 18-21

⭐ Get Ready to Read

Introduce the comprehension skill *sequencing*. Explain to students that they will read an article that tells about the history of the Iditarod, a famous sled dog race in Alaska. The events are explained in the order they happened. Ask a volunteer to read the information in the *Get Ready to Read* box. Then use Graphic Organizer 3 or draw a sequence chart on the board, similar to the one below.

Alaskans began using sled dogs around 1910 to carry supplies.

⬇

_____

⬇

_____

⬇

_____

Have students skim the top of page 19 to identify the first important date and event in the history of the Iditarod. Record their responses in the first section of the chart. Then have students set purposes for reading by asking them to look for events in the history of the Iditarod as they read. Explain that they will use these events to complete the sequence chart later.

PREVIEWING THE TEXT FEATURES

Preview the article with students. Point out one or more text features such as the photographs and the map. Model how to use these features to understand and enjoy the article:

- The photographs show what a sled dog team looks like.
- A map shows the Iditarod Trail.
- Boldfaced words show vocabulary words that can be found in the glossary.
- A diagram shows the role of each sled dog.

COMPREHENDING THE SELECTION

To promote students' fluency, pair students who are developing fluency with more proficient readers. Have them take turns reading alternate paragraphs. Point out that the *Tips* in the margins of the article help students follow the sequence of events as they read.

⭐ Tips

- You can use **dates** to help you follow the sequence, or **order**, of events.
- Season words such as **summer** and **fall** can give you clues about the order of events.
- Phrases such as **during this time** and **before the race** can help you follow the sequence of events.

After Reading the Selection

 To informally assess students' understanding, ask them to name other important events in the history of the Iditarod. Use their responses to complete the sequencing chart on Graphic Organizer 3 or on the board. (You may wish to remove the chart before students complete the Focus Skill activity.)

MEETING INDIVIDUAL NEEDS/ESL
Have students work with partners who are proficient speakers of English to describe what they see in the photographs and on the map. Encourage them to use the vocabulary words in their descriptions.

ASSESS Comprehension Check, page 22

1. **(Identifying Cause and Effect)** Have students reread the top of page 19 to locate this detail. A
2. **(Identifying Main Idea)** Remind students that a title should tell what the whole article is mainly about. F
3. **(Drawing Conclusions)** Review with students Dorothy G. Page's role in the Iditarod. D
4. **(Interpreting Graphic Sources)** Have students trace the routes on the map. G
5. **(Recalling Details)** Have students reread the top of page 21 to review this sequence. The mushers give commands to the lead dog. Then the other dogs in the team follow the lead.
6. **(Higher Level Thinking/Inferential)** Possible responses: A good driver would be someone who is in good physical shape, brave, and used to being alone. He or she must also be good with animals.

ASSESS Vocabulary Builder, page 23

Have students tell the meaning of each vocabulary word in their own words. Then have them complete page 23 independently.

Answers for Vocabulary Builder: 1. remembrance **2.** territory **3.** obstacle **4.** participate **5.** vital **6.** tundra
Extend Your Vocabulary: 7. massive **8.** muscular **9.** effective **10.** era

Focus Skill

Sequence, page 24

Ask a volunteer to read aloud the information in the instructional box. Recall with students the chart they completed earlier to record the sequence of events in the history of the Iditarod. Then have them complete the page on their own, referring to the article as needed.

Possible response:

> First, drivers must qualify for the Iditarod.

> Next, the drivers practice in the summer by having dog teams pull the sleds on the bare ground.

> Then, in January, the teams compete in practice races.

> Last, the mushers choose their lead dogs.

1. The other dogs follow the lead dog.
2. Possible response: The mushers send supplies to the race checkpoints.

Your Turn to Write, page 25

Explain to students that a sequence chart will help them write an article explaining how to do an activity they enjoy. Remind them to include all of the important steps in order and to use clue words such as *first, next, then,* and *last.*

SCORING RUBRIC

Article About an Activity
Distribute copies of the Writing Rubric Master on page 52 to students before they write.

SCORE 4 The article tells about an activity. It includes three or more steps and clue words to show the sequence. There are few or no errors in grammar, usage, and mechanics.

SCORE 3 The article tells about an activity. It includes three steps and clue words to show the sequence. There are a few errors in grammar, usage, and mechanics.

SCORE 2 The article tells about an activity. It includes two steps and uses one clue word to show the sequence. There are several errors in grammar, usage, and mechanics.

SCORE 1 The article is incomplete or does not tell about an activity. It does not include sequential steps or clue words. There are numerous errors in grammar, usage, and mechanics.

Time for Travel!

SELECTION AT A GLANCE

SYNOPSIS
This story describes how a group of children makes a trip back in time to the 1930s. Their efforts help save a family farm.

GENRE: Fiction (Science Fiction)
Explain to students that science fiction stories include details about events that could not happen in real life and include technology that has not yet been invented.

COMPREHENSION FOCUS SKILL

Making Predictions

STANDARDS

Reading
- Make and revise predictions
- Understand and distinguish literary forms such as science fiction

Vocabulary
- Know the literal meaning of words
- Use context to assign meaning to words

Writing
- Write to entertain
- Follow the conventions of punctuation, capitalization, and spelling

ADDITIONAL RESOURCES
Writing Rubric Master, page 53; Graphic Organizer 4
www.humanities-interactive.org/texas/dustbowl/

RELATED READING
Knights of the Kitchen Table (The Time Warp Trio), Jon Scieszka

Building on Background Knowledge

What Do You Already Know?

Invite students to share information they know about the Great Depression and Dust Bowl of the 1930s. Then ask a volunteer to read aloud the text under *What Do You Already Know?* on page 26. Have students discuss the questions on page 26 and the questions below.

- If you could travel back in time, what period would you want to visit? Answers will vary.
- Would you want to go back to a time that was not good for the people living then? What kinds of people might choose to go back to a time like this? Possible response: No, only people who really want to help others would want to go back to a time that was not good.
- What do you suppose happens to farmers who experience long periods of time without rain? Possible responses: Their crops fail; they might lose their farms.

VOCABULARY

abandoned   brittle   expectantly
grueling   miraculous   satchel   scouring
slogan   solitary   trudged

Introduce the content vocabulary.

- Write the vocabulary words in a column on the board. Help students make up a definition for each word, and suggest that they look up any unfamiliar words in the glossary beginning on page 106.
- Write the following words in a column next to the vocabulary words: *bag, plodded, amazing, saying, deserted, single, fragile, hopefully, scrubbing, exhausting.*
- Have students draw a line to connect each vocabulary word with its synonym. Then have students make up an original sentence for each vocabulary word.

Reading the Selection, pages 26-29

Get Ready to Read

Introduce the comprehension skill *making predictions*. Explain to students that they will read a story about time travel. As they read, they will make predictions about what will happen, based on story clues and what they already know. Ask a volunteer to read the information in the *Get Ready to Read* box. Then use Graphic Organizer 4 or draw a prediction chart on the board, similar to the one below.

Prediction
The friends will try to help the family in the article.

Story Clues That Helped Me Predict
Jim says the group tries to "make a lasting difference."

Have students read the first page of the story. Ask them to make a prediction about what will happen in the story. Then ask them what clues helped them predict. Record their ideas in the chart. Then have students set purposes for reading the story by asking them to look for other clues that help them make predictions as they read. Explain that they will complete the prediction chart later.

PREVIEWING THE TEXT FEATURES

Preview the story with students. Point out one or more text features such as the illustrations and dialogue. Model how to use these features to understand and appreciate the story:

- The illustrations give details about the characters, the setting, and events. They can also help readers predict what will happen.
- Words in quotation marks show the exact words spoken by the characters and give clues about what the characters are like.
- Boldfaced words show vocabulary words that can be found in the glossary.

COMPREHENDING THE SELECTION

To promote reading fluency, have students work in small groups. Have one student read the role of the narrator and others read the dialogue of the characters. Point out that the *Tips* in the margins of the story will help students to make better predictions as they read.

Tips

- As you read, think about what you know about the **characters** and the **setting**. Use this information to predict what will happen next in the story.
- As you continue reading, check to see if the prediction you made earlier was correct. Then **revise** your prediction if you need to.
- After you read, check your predictions. Were they correct? If not, look back and check the **story clues**.

After Reading the Selection

To informally assess students' understanding, ask them to tell some predictions they made about the story and the story clues that helped them predict. Use their responses to complete the prediction chart on Graphic Organizer 4 or on the board. (You may wish to remove the chart before students complete the Focus Skill activity.)

MEETING INDIVIDUAL NEEDS/ESL

Have students work in small groups to plan and present skits related to the story. Encourage them to pantomime the vocabulary words and other story concepts.

Possible responses:

<table>
<tr><td>Prediction
The four friends will help the farm family.</td></tr>
</table>

Story Clues That Helped Me Predict

The group's slogan is "make a lasting difference."
The friends travel back to the 1930s.
The friends bring seeds, water, and farming tools.

_____

_____

_____

ASSESS Comprehension Check, page 30

1. **(Identifying Cause and Effect)** Ask students to recall what the friends did at the library at 9:00 A.M. The children push a button on a special photocopying machine.

2. **(Identifying Setting)** Have students examine the illustrations on pages 27 and 28 and the text on page 28 for details about the setting. The farm is abandoned. The crops in the fields are dead. The inside of the house is dusty.

3. **(Distinguishing Between Realism and Fantasy)** Remind students that all science fiction includes events that could not really happen. People cannot really travel back in time with a magical copy machine.

4. **(Making Inferences)** Have students recall what the newspaper article was about. The family left because they couldn't survive on the farm.

5. **(Higher Level Thinking/Inferential)** The children plant special seeds, clean up, and repair the farm.

6. **(Higher Level Thinking/Inferential)** The slogan means that they should travel to places where they can make a difference in people's lives.

ASSESS Vocabulary Builder, page 31

Have students tell the meaning of each vocabulary word in their own words. Then have them complete page 31 independently.

Answers for Vocabulary Builder: 1. D **2.** F **3.** C **4.** H **5.** A **6.** G

Extend Your Vocabulary: 7. satchel **8.** expectantly **9.** abandoned **10.** grueling

Focus Skill

Predict, page 32

Ask a volunteer to read aloud the information in the instructional box. Recall with students the chart they began earlier to record predictions and story clues. Then have students complete the page on their own.

1. Possible response: The farm family will probably harvest their crops, plant more seeds, and be able to keep their farm.

2. Possible response: The friends will travel to another time and place to help other people.

Your Turn to Write, page 33

Explain to students that a prediction chart will help them write a story about traveling back in time. Remind them to include clues that can help readers make predictions about what happens as the story unfolds.

SCORING RUBRIC

Story About Time Travel
Distribute copies of the Writing Rubric Master on page 53 to students before they write.

 The story tells about traveling back in time and includes details about where the writer would go and what he or she would do. It includes three clues that would help readers predict. There are few or no errors in grammar, usage, and mechanics.

 The story tells about traveling back in time and includes details about where the writer would go and what he or she would do. It includes two clues that would help readers predict. There are a few errors in grammar, usage, and mechanics.

 The story tells about traveling back in time and includes few details about where the writer would go and what he or she would do. It lacks clues that would help readers predict. There are several errors in grammar, usage, and mechanics.

 The story is incomplete or does not tell about traveling back in time. It lacks details about where the writer would go and what he or she would do. It is missing clues that would help readers predict. There are numerous errors in grammar, usage, and mechanics.

MAKING PREDICTIONS

5 Creatures of the Deep

Student Book pages 34–41

SELECTION AT A GLANCE

SYNOPSIS
The article describes four creatures that inhabit the deepest part of oceans and explains how they have adapted to this unusual environment.

GENRE: Nonfiction (Science Article)
Remind students that nonfiction articles provide factual information on a particular topic. Some science articles describe living things in a particular habitat.

COMPREHENSION FOCUS SKILL
Comparing and Contrasting

STANDARDS
Reading
- Connect, compare, and contrast ideas, themes, and issues
- Use organizational features of texts such as glossaries, diagrams, and subheadings

Vocabulary
- Use context to assign meaning to words
- Extend awareness of similes

Writing
- Write to inform and describe
- Follow the conventions of punctuation, capitalization, and spelling

Science
- Life Science: Characteristics of organisms; Organisms and environments

ADDITIONAL RESOURCES
Writing Rubric Master, page 54; Graphic Organizer 5
www.panda.org/kids/wildlife

RELATED READING
The Living Ocean, Steck-Vaughn *Pair-It Books* Proficiency Stage 6

Building on Background Knowledge

What Do You Already Know?
Tap into students' prior knowledge by asking a volunteer to read aloud the text under *What Do You Already Know?* on page 34. Then have students discuss the questions that are on page 34 and the questions below.

- What do you think it is like very deep in the ocean? Can people explore there? Why or why not? Possible responses: Deep in the ocean, the water is cold and dark. The cold water, darkness, and depth might make exploration very difficult.
- What kind of sea life makes its home deep in the ocean? Possible response: interesting fish

VOCABULARY

abdomen	afloat	bacteria	compete	digest
hostile	lures	microscopic	mobile	penetrate

Introduce the content vocabulary by using the following "Word Web" technique.

- Write the vocabulary words on the board and help students make up a definition for each one. Have them look up any unfamiliar words in the glossary beginning on page 106.
- Begin a word web on the board. Write the words *deep ocean* in the center. Explain to students that the article they will read describes several types of fish that share a habitat very deep in the ocean.
- Ask students to suggest ways that the vocabulary words might relate to a deep-sea habitat. Use their responses to complete the web.
- Save the web for students to review after they have read the selection.

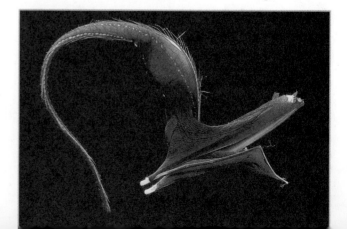

Reading the Selection, pages 34-37

Get Ready to Read

Introduce the comprehension skill *comparing and contrasting*. Explain to students that they will read an article that compares and contrasts several kinds of fish that live deep in the ocean. Ask a volunteer to read the information in the *Get Ready to Read* box. Then use Graphic Organizer 5 or draw a Venn diagram on the board, similar to the one below.

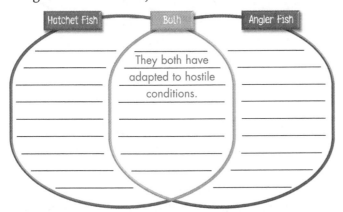

Hatchet Fish | Both | Angler Fish

They both have adapted to hostile conditions.

Have students read page 34 to find one way that all deep-sea creatures are alike. Record their responses in the center of the Venn diagram. Then have students set purposes for reading the article by asking them to look for other similarities and differences among the fish described in the article. Explain to students that they will use these details to complete the Venn diagram later.

PREVIEWING THE TEXT FEATURES

Preview the article with students. Point out one or more text features such as the subheads, labels, and the photographs. Model how to use these features to understand and appreciate the article:

- The photographs show the deep-sea fish described in the article.
- Labels tell what is shown in the photographs.
- Subheads suggest the main idea of each section.
- Boldfaced words show vocabulary words that can be found in the glossary.

COMPREHENDING THE SELECTION

To promote students' fluency, tape-record a fluent reading of the article. Have students listen to the recording and then read along with it. Point out that the *Tips* in the margins of the article give clue words and phrases that show comparisons and contrasts.

Tips

- Words such as **all**, **both**, and **like** show that things are being compared.
- Words such as **fewer**, **less**, and **slower** show that things are being contrasted.
- The phrase **on the other hand** tells you that things are being contrasted. Other contrast words include **unlike**, **but**, and **however**.

After Reading the Selection

ASSESS To informally assess students' understanding, ask them to tell a few similarities and differences between the hatchet fish and the angler fish. Use their responses to complete the Venn diagram on Graphic Organizer 5 or on the board. (You may wish to remove the diagram before students complete the Focus Skill activity.)

MEETING INDIVIDUAL NEEDS/ESL

Have students of varying language abilities work in a group to create a deep-sea mural. Have them add labels that name and describe the fish on the mural.

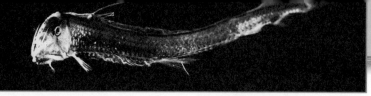

 Comprehension Check, page 38

1. **(Identifying Main Idea)** Remind students that a main idea statement tells what the article is mainly about. C
2. **(Summarizing)** Have students identify what makes the deep-sea habitat different from other parts of the ocean. F
3. **(Distinguishing Fact from Opinion)** Remind students that facts can be proven. An opinion is what someone thinks or believes. D
4. **(Recalling Details)** Have students recall how gulper eels lure their prey. G
5. **(Higher Level Thinking/Inferential)** Possible response: Deep-sea fish have soft bodies so they can withstand the water pressure.
6. **(Higher Level Thinking/Inferential)** Possible response: Since there are so few angler fish, the male might never find a mate if he didn't find a female in the batch of baby fish.

 Vocabulary Builder, page 39

Have students recall the word web they began before reading. Ask them to add any new ideas to show how the words relate to a deep-sea habitat. Then have students tell the meaning of each vocabulary word in their own words and complete page 39 on their own.

Answers for Vocabulary Builder: 1. afloat **2.** bacteria **3.** lures **4.** penetrate **5.** abdomen **6.** digest **7.** compete **Extend Your Vocabulary: 8.** microscopic **9.** hostile **10.** mobile

Compare and Contrast, page 40
Ask a volunteer to read aloud the information in the instructional box. Recall with students the Venn diagram they began before reading to note similarities and differences among deep-sea fish. Then have them complete the page on their own, referring to the article as needed.

Possible responses:

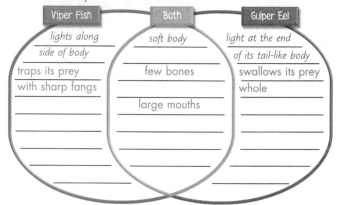

Viper Fish	Both	Gulper Eel
lights along side of body	soft body	light at the end of its tail-like body
traps its prey with sharp fangs	few bones	swallows its prey whole
	large mouths	

1. Both have lighted body parts, soft bodies, few bones, and huge fangs.
2. They have lights in different places and eat different foods.

 Your Turn to Write, page 41
Explain to students that a Venn diagram will help them write an article that compares and contrasts two animals. Encourage them to use clue words such as *both*, *all*, and *like* to show similarities and *unlike* and *but* to show differences.

SCORING RUBRIC

Article That Compares and Contrasts
Distribute copies of the Writing Rubric Master on page 54 to students before they write.

 The article compares and contrasts two animals. It includes at least two similarities and two differences. It uses clue words. There are few or no errors in grammar, usage, and mechanics.

 The article compares and contrasts two animals. It includes two similarities and/or differences. It uses a few clue words. There are a few errors in grammar, usage, and mechanics.

 The article compares and contrasts two animals. It includes one similarity or one difference. It uses one or two clue words. There are several errors in grammar, usage, and mechanics.

 The article is incomplete. It does not describe two animals, or it lacks details about similarities or differences. It uses no clue words. There are numerous errors in grammar, usage, and mechanics.

The Greatest Trip Ever

Student Book pages 42–49

SELECTION AT A GLANCE

SYNOPSIS

Ashley thinks she has seen everything as she heads off for a camping trip with her family and a friend. A surprise awaits her, though: the fantastic Northern Lights.

GENRE: Fiction (Realistic Story)

Explain to students that in realistic stories the characters and the things that happen to them are similar to people and events that happen in real life.

COMPREHENSION FOCUS SKILL

Making Inferences

STANDARDS

Reading

- Draw inferences such as conclusions or generalizations and support them with text evidence and experience

Vocabulary

- Know the literal meaning of words
- Use context to assign meaning to words

Writing

- Create multiple-paragraph narrative compositions including developing a situation or plot, setting, and ending

ADDITIONAL RESOURCES

Writing Rubric Master, page 55; Graphic Organizer 6
ksnn.larc.nasa.gov/northernlights.html

RELATED READING

Northern Lights (Nature in Action), Dorothy Souza

Building on Background Knowledge

What Do You Already Know?

Tap into students' prior knowledge about camping trips by asking a volunteer to read aloud the text under *What Do You Already Know?* on page 42. Then have students discuss the questions on page 42 and the questions below.

- What do you like or think you would like best and least about camping? Answers will vary.
- Have you ever been camping some place far away from cities? What did the night sky look like? Possible response: clear, very starry

VOCABULARY

arc   campsite   companion   exasperated
extraordinary   horizon   landscape
mouthwatering   secretive   solar

Introduce the content vocabulary by using the following "Prediction" technique.

- List the vocabulary words on the board. Help students make up a definition for each word, and suggest that they look up any unfamiliar words in the glossary beginning on page 106.
- Tell students that they will read a story about a girl who takes a camping trip with her family and a friend. Have students read the vocabulary words and make predictions about how the words will be used in the story.
- Record their responses on a three-column chart. The first column should list the vocabulary words; the second and third columns should have the headings "My Prediction" and "How It Is Used in the Story," respectively.

Reading the Selection, pages 42–45

Get Ready to Read

Introduce the comprehension skill *making infer-ences*. Explain that sometimes readers must use what they know to make sense of a character's actions or story events when the writer does not provide all the details about it. Ask a volunteer to read the information in the *Get Ready to Read* box. Then use Graphic Organizer 6 or draw an inference chart on the board, similar to the one below.

Inference

Ashley has been camping in Vermont before.

Supporting Details

She knows that a red barn marks the halfway point in their trip.

Have students read the first page and tell what they can infer about Ashley. Record their ideas in the inference section of the chart. Then ask them to identify the clue or clues that helped them make this inference. Write their suggestions on the chart in the *Supporting Details* section. Have students set purposes for reading by asking them to note what other inferences they can make. Explain that they will complete the inference chart later.

PREVIEWING THE TEXT FEATURES

Preview the story with students. Point out one or more text features such as the illustrations, dialogue, and a photograph. Model how to use these features to understand and enjoy the story:

- Words in quotation marks show the exact words spoken by the characters and give clues about what they are like.
- The photograph on page 46 shows what the Northern Lights actually look like.
- Boldfaced words show vocabulary words that can be found in the glossary.

COMPREHENDING THE SELECTION

To promote reading fluency, pair a student who is developing fluency with one who is already a fluent reader. Have them reread the story, taking turns reading alternate pages. Point out that the *Tips* in the margins of the story help students make inferences as they read.

Tips

- What a character **says** or **does** can help you make inferences about what he or she is thinking.
- You can use **your own experiences** to make inferences about how characters feel.
- A character's **actions** can help you make inferences.

After Reading the Selection

ASSESS To informally assess students' understanding, ask them to tell an inference they made as they read the story and some clues that helped them make this inference. Record their responses on the inference chart on Graphic Organizer 6 or on the board. (You may wish to remove the chart before students complete the Focus Skill activity.)

MEETING INDIVIDUAL NEEDS/ESL

Have students role-play parts of the story, each taking the part of a story character. They can read dialogue as they act out the events, or make up words of their own.

ASSESS Comprehension Check, page 46

1. **(Summarizing)** Tell students to state the main events of the story in a single sentence. The story is about a family and friend who go on a camping trip and see the Northern Lights.

2. **(Identifying Setting)** Tell students that the story illustrations can help them review the different settings. The story takes place first in the family car and then at a campsite in Vermont.

3. **(Sequencing)** Have students look for clue words at the top of page 44. The family finds their campsite and sets up their tents.

4. **(Analyzing Characters)** Have students examine Ashley's words and actions. Ashley is excited. She looks forward to the trip every summer.

5. **(Higher Level Thinking/Inferential)** Mrs. Mayer knows that Ashley and Ken will see the Northern Lights later and is looking forward to surprising them.

6. **(Higher Level Thinking/Inferential)** The author uses vivid descriptions, such as "curtains of red and purple."

ASSESS Vocabulary Builder, page 47

Have students complete the vocabulary chart they began before reading by noting how the words were used in the story. Then have them compare the entries in this column to their predictions. Have students complete page 47 independently.

Answers for Vocabulary Builder: 1. A **2.** F **3.** D
4. G **5.** A **6.** F
Extend Your Vocabulary: 7. mouthwatering
8. extraordinary **9.** landscape **10.** campsite

Make Inferences, page 48

Ask a volunteer to read aloud the information in the instructional box. Recall with students the chart they began earlier. Then have them complete the page on their own, referring to the story as needed.

Possible response:

Inference
Ashley has never seen the Northern Lights before.

Supporting Details
Ashley's parents say there will be a surprise on the trip.
Her mother says that she may see some new colors.
Her father hints that she hasn't seen everything yet.

1. Ken doesn't have much camping experience. He doesn't know how to set up his tent or fish.

2. Ashley's family has gone camping for many years. Ashley remembers all the details of the trip.

 Your Turn to Write, page 49

Explain to students that an inference chart will help them write about something special that happens on a familiar trip. Remind them to include details that will help readers make inferences.

SCORING RUBRIC

Story About a Familiar Trip
Distribute copies of the Writing Rubric Master on page 55 to students before they write.

 The story tells about a surprising event that happens on a familiar trip. It includes several details that allow readers to form one or more inferences. There are no errors in grammar, usage, and mechanics.

 The story tells about a surprising event that happens on a familiar trip. The story includes a few details that allow readers to make an inference. There are a few errors in grammar, usage, and mechanics.

 The story tells about a surprising event that happens on a familiar trip. The story lacks details that allow readers to make an inference. There are several errors in grammar, usage, and mechanics.

 The story is incomplete or does not tell about something surprising that happens on a familiar trip. It is lacking details and there are numerous errors in grammar, usage, and mechanics.

REVIEW

The Tomb of Emperor Qin Shi Huangdi

SYNOPSIS

This article tells about the tomb of Emperor Qin Shi Huangdi, who ruled China from about 221 to 210 BC. The contents of the tomb provide many clues about life in ancient China.

GENRE: Nonfiction (Social Studies Article)

Remind students that a nonfiction article gives facts and information about a topic.

COMPREHENSION FOCUS SKILLS

Sequencing

Comparing and Contrasting

Identifying Main Idea and Supporting Details

Making Inferences

Making Predictions

Reviewing the Comprehension Skills

Review the following comprehension skills, which are presented in this article.

- **Sequencing:** The sequence of events is the order in which things happen.
- **Comparing and Contrasting:** Comparing means telling how two or more things are alike. Contrasting means telling how they are different.
- **Identifying Main Idea/Supporting Details:** The main idea is the most important idea in an article. The supporting details give more information about the main idea.
- **Making Inferences:** Sometimes you must make decisions, or inferences, about information that is not stated directly in an article. You can use clues and what you already know.
- **Making Predictions:** When you predict, you guess what will happen next. Story clues can help you predict.

Reading the Selection, page 50

 Get Ready to Read

Have students set purposes for reading by asking them to read the title of the article and look at the photograph and the map. Then have volunteers predict what the article will be about. Ask students to read to see whether their predictions were correct.

After Reading the Selection, page 51

ASSESS Comprehension Check

1. **(Sequencing)** Ask students to recall the discovery of the tomb. C
2. **(Comparing and Contrasting)** Have students reread the second paragraph of the article. E
3. **(Identifying Main Idea)** Have students tell what this article is mostly about. D
4. **(Comparing and Contrasting)** Have students review what they know about the clay figures. H
5. **(Identifying Main Idea)** Possible response: We can learn a lot about ancient China by studying the tomb of Emperor Qin Shi Huangdi.
6. **(Making Inferences)** Possible response: It probably took a long time to build the tomb because there were so many detailed figures inside.
7. **(Making Predictions)** Possible response: They will discover more figures and continue learning about ancient China.

 MEETING INDIVIDUAL NEEDS/ESL

To help students compare and contrast, invite them to read back through the article and name facts about the clay and ceramic figures found in Qin Shi Huangdi's tomb. List their responses on the board in a two-column chart with the headings *Clay Figures* and *Ceramic Figures*. Ask volunteers to underline the facts that are repeated in both columns. Explain that this shows ways the clay and ceramic figures are alike. Then ask students to use the chart to tell how the figures are alike and how they are different.

Student Book pages 52–53

An Unexpected Discovery

SYNOPSIS
In this story, Maya and John discover an unusual bone near their driveway. Maya suspects it may be a dinosaur bone, so the children take it to a local dinosaur expert to see whether it is.

GENRE: Fiction (Realistic Story)
Remind students that a realistic story contains characters and events like those in real life.

COMPREHENSION FOCUS SKILLS
Sequencing

Analyzing Characters

Making Predictions

Making Inferences

Reviewing the Comprehension Skills

Review the following comprehension skills, which are presented in this story.

- **Sequencing:** The sequence of events is the order in which things happen.
- **Analyzing Characters:** Characters are the people in a fiction story. You can learn about characters from what they say and do, as well as from what other characters say or feel about them.
- **Making Predictions:** When you predict, you guess what will happen next in a story. You can make a prediction by using story clues in the text and what you already know.
- **Making Inferences:** Sometimes you must make decisions, or inferences, about information that is not stated directly in a story. You can use clues from the story, along with what you already know, to make inferences.

Reading the Selection, page 52

Get Ready to Read
Have students set purposes for reading. Ask them to read the title of the story and look at the illustration. Then have volunteers predict what they think the story is about. Ask students to read to see whether their predictions were correct.

After Reading the Selection, page 53

ASSESS Comprehension Check

1. **(Sequencing)** Have students review the order of events in the story. B
2. **(Analyzing Characters)** Have students recall what John says about the bone. F
3. **(Sequencing)** Have students recall what Maya suggested as she looked at the bone. A
4. **(Making Predictions)** Have students tell what they would do next if they were Maya or John. G
5. **(Making Inferences)** Possible response: I can infer that Maya and John live near the park because they were able to bicycle there.
6. **(Making Inferences)** Possible response: People will know for sure that the Dilophosaurus came to Connecticut.
7. **(Analyzing Characters)** Possible response: I think Maya is smart because she knew that the bone might have come from a dinosaur and that dinosaur tracks had been found at a nearby park. I also think she doesn't give up easily, because she convinced John to go to the park with her.

MEETING INDIVIDUAL NEEDS/ESL
To help students analyze the story characters, divide the class into groups of three—one student for each character—to act out story events. Encourage students to use gestures and facial expressions to highlight their characters' words and actions.

LESSON 7 — Welcome to Hawaii!

Student Book pages 54–61

SELECTION AT A GLANCE

SYNOPSIS
Hawaii is a string of islands formed by volcanoes in the Pacific Ocean. This article invites readers to explore Hawaii and discover what makes it a great vacation spot.

GENRE: Nonfiction (Social Studies Article)
Explain to students that a nonfiction article gives factual information about a particular topic. It may also express the author's opinions.

COMPREHENSION FOCUS SKILL
Distinguishing Fact from Opinion

STANDARDS
Reading
- Distinguish facts and opinions in texts

Vocabulary
- Use a variety of strategies to determine meaning and increase vocabulary such as synonyms and word relationships
- Use root words and affixes to analyze the meaning of complex words

Writing
- Write an expository description
- Follow the conventions of punctuation, capitalization, and spelling

Social Studies
- People, Places, and Environments: Locate and distinguish among varying landforms and geographic features

ADDITIONAL RESOURCES
Writing Rubric Master, page 56; Graphic Organizer 7
gohawaii.about.com/library/weekly/aa020199.htm

RELATED READING
Hawaii (From Sea to Shining Sea), Dennis Brindell Fradin

Building on Background Knowledge

? What Do You Already Know?
Tap into students' prior knowledge by asking a volunteer to read aloud the text under *What Do You Already Know?* on page 54. Then discuss with students the questions on page 54 and the questions below.

- Have you ever visited Hawaii? What do you think you might see and do if you were visiting Hawaii? Possible responses: a group of islands in the Pacific Ocean; a place with great beaches, surfing, volcanoes, and friendly people
- What do you think Hawaii's climate is like? Possible responses: warm, pleasant, mild, sunny

VOCABULARY

accessible   balmy   dormant   eruption
inhabitants   lei   magnificent   petroglyphs
sulfur   variations

Introduce the content vocabulary.

- List the vocabulary words on the board and help students generate a definition for each word. Have them look up any unfamiliar words in the glossary beginning on page 106.
- Have students discuss the sentences and questions below to extend their understanding of the vocabulary words.
  1. How would you wear a lei?
  2. Name some natural wonders that you think are magnificent.
  3. What can you describe as balmy?
  4. Where might you see petroglyphs?
  5. Name something that can be dormant.
  6. How can you tell if something is accessible?
  7. Describe what happens when sulfur burns.
  8. What are the inhabitants of Hawaii called?
  9. Name some things that can have variations.
  10. Describe an eruption you have read about or observed.

DISTINGUISHING FACT FROM OPINION

Reading the Selection, pages 54-57

Get Ready to Read

Introduce the comprehension skill *distinguishing fact from opinion*. Explain to students that the article they will read includes both facts and opinions about Hawaii. Ask a volunteer to read the information in the *Get Ready to Read* box. Use Graphic Organizer 7 or draw a fact-and-opinion chart on the board, similar to the one below.

Facts	Opinions
Aloha is the Hawaiian word for "love."	Everything you need for a great vacation is right here.

Have students read the first paragraph to find a sentence that includes a fact and a sentence that includes an opinion. Record their ideas in the chart. Then have students set purposes for reading by asking them to find other facts and opinions about Hawaii. Explain that they will use this information to complete the fact-and-opinion chart after they read the article.

PREVIEWING THE TEXT FEATURES

Preview the article with students. Point out one or more text features in the article such as the photographs, subheads, and map. Model how to use these features to understand and appreciate the article:

- The photographs show some of the sights that visitors can see in Hawaii.
- The subheads show what each section is about.
- The map shows the Hawaiian Islands.
- Boldfaced words show vocabulary words that can be found in the glossary.

COMPREHENDING THE SELECTION

To promote fluency, have individual students take turns reading the article one-on-one with you, a classroom aid, or with another student who can provide a model of fluent reading, help with word recognition, and provide feedback. Point out that the *Tips* in the margins of the article can help students distinguish facts from opinions as they read.

Tips

- To find opinions, look for words that show beliefs or feelings such as **beautiful**, **great**, **perfect**, and **interesting**.
- As you read a statement, ask yourself, "Can this be **proven** to be true?" If the answer is "yes," then the statement is a fact.
- You can check a **source**, such as an encyclopedia or atlas, to find out if a fact is true or accurate.

After Reading the Selection

ASSESS To informally assess students' understanding, ask them to identify some facts and opinions in the article and explain how they know the difference. Use their responses to complete the fact-and-opinion chart on the board or on Graphic Organizer 7. (You may wish to remove the chart before students complete the Focus Skill activity.)

MEETING INDIVIDUAL NEEDS/ESL

Write the words *eruption*, *dormant*, *sulfur*, and *variations* on the board. Then display photographs of an active volcano before, during, and after its most recent eruption. Guide students to use the vocabulary words to describe and compare and contrast the volcano in the photographs.

Comprehension Check, page 58

1. **(Identifying Author's Purpose)** Review common author's purposes for writing. D
2. **(Visualizing)** Have students note details that help them picture Hawaii. G
3. **(Identifying Cause and Effect)** Ask students to recall the sport that was invented by the first inhabitants of the Hawaiian Islands and why Oahu is a perfect place for it. D
4. **(Drawing Conclusions)** Ask students to discuss how the weather varies in Hawaii. G
5. **(Higher Level Thinking/Inferential)** Possible responses: The author thinks Hawaii is a wonderful place to visit. You can tell because the author uses words such as *beautiful* and *magnificent* to describe it. The author also encourages readers to visit the islands.
6. **(Higher Level Thinking/Inferential)** Answers will vary.

Vocabulary Builder, page 59

Have students review the meanings of the vocabulary words and the discussion they had before they read the story. Then have students complete page 59 independently.

Answers for Vocabulary Builder: 1. petroglyphs **2.** lei **3.** variations **4.** sulfur **5.** magnificent **6.** balmy **7.** dormant **8.** inhabitants
Extend Your Vocabulary: 9. access(ible), able to be accessed easily **10.** erup(t)(tion), the act or state of erupting

Fact and Opinion, page 60

Ask a volunteer to read aloud the information in the instructional box. Recall with students the chart they used earlier to note facts and opinions from the article. Then have them complete the page independently, referring to the article as needed.

Possible response:

Facts	Opinions
A lei is a native Hawaiian tradition.	Hawaii's islands are magnificent.
Hawaii is a string of islands in the Pacific Ocean.	Hawaii has perfect beaches, interesting history, and friendly people.
The Hawaiian islands were formed by volcanoes.	Everything you need for a perfect vacation is right here.
Two of Hawaii's volcanoes are active.	Hawaii is the perfect destination.
Hilo is the rainiest city in the United States.	Petroglyphs are fascinating.

1. Answers will vary.   **2.** Answers will vary.

Your Turn to Write, page 61

Explain to students that a fact-and-opinion chart will help them write an article for a travel magazine about a place they know well. Have them write an article that includes both facts and opinions and to include words and phrases that highlight opinions.

SCORING RUBRIC

Article for a Travel Magazine
Distribute copies of the Writing Rubric Master on page 56 to students before they write.

SCORE 4 The article focuses on a place the student knows well and has strong feelings about. The article includes more than two facts and more than two opinions, and uses two or more words or phrases to highlight opinions. There are no errors in grammar, usage, and mechanics.

SCORE 3 The article focuses on a place that the student knows well. The article includes two facts and two opinions. It includes one or two words or phrases to highlight opinions. There are a few errors in grammar, usage, and mechanics.

SCORE 2 The article shows little focus on a place of interest to the student. The article states one fact and one opinion. It has one word or phrase to highlight the opinion. There are several errors in grammar, usage, and mechanics.

SCORE 1 The article is unfocused or does not focus on the topic. The article is missing facts or opinions, or both. It does not include words or phrases to highlight opinions. There are numerous errors in grammar, usage, and mechanics.

Student Book pages 62–69

SELECTION AT A GLANCE

SYNOPSIS
Paolo secretly dreams that Mario, the best puppet maker in Olinda, Brazil, will spot one of his masks during the Carnaval parade and ask him to become his apprentice. Then Paolo accidentally damages a mask he had been working on. Can Paolo fix it in time for the parade?

GENRE: Fiction (Realistic Story)
Explain to students that in a realistic story the characters and the things that happen to them are similar to people and events that happen in real life. The main character's problem and its solution form the story's plot.

COMPREHENSION FOCUS SKILL

Identifying Plot

STANDARDS

Reading
- Recognize and analyze story plot, setting, and problem resolution
- Analyze characters, including their motivations and conflicts

Vocabulary
- Understand the literal meaning of words
- Draw on experiences to bring meanings to words in context such as interpreting multiple-meaning words

Writing
- Create multiple-paragraph narrative compositions including developing a situation or plot, setting, and ending

ADDITIONAL RESOURCES
Writing Rubric Master, page 57; Graphic Organizer 8
www.quatrocantos.com/carnaval_de_olinda/

RELATED READING
Carnaval, George Ancona

Building on Background Knowledge

What Do You Already Know?
Tap into students' prior knowledge by asking a volunteer to read aloud the text under *What Do You Already Know?* on page 62. Then discuss with students the questions on page 62 and the questions below.

- What holidays do we often celebrate with parades in our country? Possible responses: Independence Day, Thanksgiving, Mardi Gras
- Why are parades important? Possible response: They give people a chance to get together and celebrate.
- Have you ever heard of a celebration called Carnaval? Where is Carnaval celebrated? How? Answers will vary.
- What word in English is very similar to *Carnaval*? What do they both refer to? Possible response: *Carnival*; they both refer to festivities and social gatherings.

VOCABULARY

> apprentice   castanets   elaborate   gauze
> gruesome   hamper   painstaking   protruded
> racket   standstill

Introduce the content vocabulary.

- Write the vocabulary words on the board. Help students make up a definition for each word, and have them look up any unfamiliar words in the glossary beginning on page 106.
- Write the following groups of words on the board. Have volunteers identify a vocabulary word that fits with each group.
1. hinder, impede, hamper
2. thorough, careful, painstaking
3. halt, stop, standstill
4. complex, intricate, elaborate
5. learner, trainee, apprentice
6. horrible, shocking, gruesome
7. stuck out, extended, protruded
8. noise, commotion, racket
9. bandage, material, gauze
10. cymbals, triangles, castanets

Reading the Selection, pages 62–65

Get Ready to Read

Introduce the comprehension skill *identifying plot*. Explain to students that this story takes place during Carnaval, a special festival celebrated in Brazil. Ask a volunteer to read the information in the *Get Ready to Read* box. Then use Graphic Organizer 8 or draw a plot chart on the board, similar to the one below.

> **Beginning**
> Paolo helped his uncle make masks for Carnaval.
>
> ▼
>
> **Middle**
> _____
> _____
> _____
>
> ▼
>
> **End**
> _____
> _____
> _____

Have students look at the illustration on page 63 and read the second paragraph to find out what happens at the beginning of the story. Record their responses in the "beginning" section of the chart. Then have students set purposes for reading by asking them to find out what happens in the middle and at the end of the story. Explain that they will use this information to complete the plot chart after they read.

PREVIEWING THE TEXT FEATURES

Preview the story with students. Point out one or more special features such as the illustrations, the use of quotation marks, and the boldfaced words. Model how to use these features to understand and enjoy the story:

- The illustrations show how people celebrate Carnaval in Olinda and what the masks look like, as well as important events in the story.
- Remind students that the quotation marks identify the exact words of different characters.
- Boldfaced words show vocabulary words that can be found in the glossary.

COMPREHENDING THE SELECTION

To help students enhance their fluency, have small groups of students read this story as a reader's theater piece. Point out that the *Tips* in the margins of the story give information about the story plot: what problem the main character has and how it is solved by the end of the story.

Tips

- As you read, ask yourself, "What **problem** does the main character have?"
- As you continue reading, ask yourself, "How will the character's problem be **solved**?"
- At the end of the story, go back over the plot. First recall the character's **problem**. Then ask yourself how the problem was **solved**.

After Reading the Selection

ASSESS To informally assess the students' understanding, ask students to tell the important things that happened at the beginning, middle, and end of the story. Use their responses to complete the plot chart on the board or on Graphic Organizer 8. (You may wish to remove the chart before students complete the Focus Skill activity.)

MEETING INDIVIDUAL NEEDS/ESL

Write the words *painstaking* and *standstill* on the board, noting that both are compound words because they are made up of two words. Ask volunteers to identify the two words in each compound word and draw a line between them. Discuss how to use the meanings of the smaller words to figure out the meaning of each compound word.

Comprehension Check, page 66

1. **(Identifying Setting)** Ask students to review page 62 to recall where the story takes place. The story takes place in Olinda, Brazil.

2. **(Comparing and Contrasting)** Have students look at the illustrations and describe how the people are celebrating Carnaval in Olinda. In other Brazilian cities, people parade through the streets on floats. In Olinda, people carry huge puppets.

3. **(Analyzing Character)** Have students recall Paolo's secret dream. Paolo wants to make his masks special so that the master puppet maker will notice them.

4. **(Identifying Cause and Effect)** Have students recall what Uncle José is famous for. Uncle José doesn't want Paolo to paint the donkey mask pink because he is famous for his gray donkeys.

5. **(Higher Level Thinking/Inferential)** Have students recall what Paolo does after damaging the mask. Paolo is determined to achieve his dream despite any setbacks.

6. **(Higher Level Thinking/Inferential)** Have students tell what Mario says when he sees the bear with the pink bandage and white gauze. Paolo will apprentice with Mario and learn to make the giant puppets.

 Vocabulary Builder, page 67

Have students review the meanings of the vocabulary words. Then have them complete page 67 independently.

Answers for Vocabulary Builder: 1. B **2.** E **3.** A **4.** G **5.** C **6.** E **7.** D **8.** H
Extend Your Vocabulary: 9. d **10.** b **11.** c **12.** a

Plot, page 68

Have a volunteer read aloud the information in the instructional box on page 68. Recall with students how they used a plot chart to record what happened in the beginning, middle, and end of the story. Then have them complete the page independently, referring to the story as needed.

Possible response:

Beginning
Paolo helped his uncle make masks for Carnaval.

Middle
Paolo danced around in his bear mask and damaged it.

End
Paolo paraded in his bandaged mask. The puppet maker noticed the funny mask and asked Paolo to work for him.

1. Paolo damages his mask for Carnaval.
2. Paolo paints on a bandage and glues on gauze. The master puppet maker sees the repaired mask and thinks it is funny.

Your Turn to Write, page 69

Explain to students that a plot chart will help them plan a new story about Paolo that takes place at next year's Carnaval. Have students make notes about the beginning, middle, and end of their story. Remind them to include a problem and a solution and to tell about the events in order.

SCORING RUBRIC

Story About Paolo
Distribute copies of the Writing Rubric Master on page 57 to students before they write.

SCORE 4 The story is about Paolo and takes place at next year's Carnaval. The story has a clear beginning, middle, and end. It also has a clear problem and a solution, and the events are told in sequential order. There are no errors in grammar, usage, and mechanics.

SCORE 3 The story is about Paolo, but it may not take place at next year's Carnaval. The order of events is fairly clear and easy to follow. The story includes a problem and a solution. There are a few errors in grammar, usage, and mechanics.

SCORE 2 The story is about Paolo, but it does not focus on next year's Carnaval. The story shows some organization and a problem and a solution. There are several errors in grammar, usage, and mechanics.

SCORE 1 The story fails to tell about Paolo or Carnaval. The sequence of events is difficult to follow. The story does not have a problem or solution. There are many errors in grammar, usage, and mechanics.

JIM ABBOTT: GREAT ATHLETE, GREAT MAN

Student Book pages 70–77

SELECTION AT A GLANCE

SYNOPSIS
Jim Abbott was born with only one hand, but it did not prevent him from becoming a major-league pitcher. His determination has made him a great athlete and a role model.

GENRE: Nonfiction (Biography)
Explain to students that a biography tells about the life of a real person. It may cover a person's entire life or just some of the highlights.

COMPREHENSION FOCUS SKILL
Summarizing

STANDARDS
Reading
• Paraphrase and summarize text to recall, inform, or organize ideas

Vocabulary
• Use context to assign meaning to an unknown word
• Use a variety of strategies to increase vocabulary, such as synonyms

Writing
• Write to inform
• Follow the conventions of punctuation, capitalization, and spelling

Social Studies
• Individual Development and Identity: Relate such factors as physical capabilities and motivation to individual development

ADDITIONAL RESOURCES
Writing Rubric Master, page 58; Graphic Organizer 9
www.pubdim.net/baseballlibrary/ballplayers

RELATED READING
Jim Abbott: Star Pitcher (Millbrook Sports World), Bill Gutman

Building on Background Knowledge

What Do You Already Know?
Tap into students' prior knowledge by asking a volunteer to read aloud the text under *What Do You Already Know?* on page 70. Discuss the question on page 70 and the questions below.

• Who are some outstanding athletes that you know about? Do you think they make good role models? Why or why not? Responses will vary.
• Why do you think people like to read biographies? Possible response: It is interesting to read about the important events in a person's life.

VOCABULARY

amateur astounded bunt determination
disabled excelled ovation pinnacle
progressively technique

Introduce the content vocabulary.

• List the vocabulary words on the board. Help students generate a definition for each word, and have them look up any unfamiliar words in the glossary beginning on page 106.
• Ask students to identify the word or words that fit clues such as the following:
1. A word that tells what someone might teach to others bunt, technique
2. A word that tells what someone did excelled, astounded
3. A word that tells what someone might reach pinnacle
4. A word that can tell the status of an athlete amateur
5. A word that can describe a person astounded, disabled, amateur
6. A word that tells what a person might receive from others ovation
7. A word that tells how someone or something moves progressively
8. A word that tells what a person might feel if he or she does not want to give up determination

SUMMARIZING

Reading the Selection, pages 70-73

⭐ Get Ready to Read

Introduce the comprehension skill *summarizing*. Explain to students that they will read a biography that shows how Jim Abbott overcame a disability to become a major-league pitcher and role model. Ask a volunteer to read aloud the information in the *Get Ready to Read* box. Then use Graphic Organizer 9 or draw a summary chart on the board, similar to the one below.

JIM ABBOTT
GREAT ATHLETE, GREAT MAN

MOST IMPORTANT IDEA OF PAGE 70	MOST IMPORTANT IDEA OF PAGE 71
Jim Abbott overcame problems to achieve his dreams.	
MOST IMPORTANT IDEA OF PAGE 72	**MOST IMPORTANT IDEA OF PAGE 73**

Have students read page 70 to find the page's most important idea. Record their ideas in the *Most Important Idea of Page 70* box of the chart. Then have students set purposes for reading by asking them to find the most important ideas of the remaining sections of the biography. Explain that they will use this information to complete the summary chart after they read.

PREVIEWING THE TEXT FEATURES

Preview the biography and point out some of its text features such as the photographs and the timeline. Model the use of these features to understand and enjoy the biography:

- The photographs show how Jim Abbott pitches.
- The baseball card shows Jim Abbott's major-league statistics.
- The timeline shows many of Jim Abbott's career highlights.
- Boldfaced words show vocabulary words that can be found in the glossary.

COMPREHENDING THE SELECTION

Promote students' reading fluency by having them reread parts of the article individually. Point out that the *Tips* in the margins of the article show how to identify the most important ideas in order to summarize.

⭐ Tips

- A summary includes only the **most important** ideas and details. As you read, ask yourself, "What are the most important ideas?"
- Look at the **subheads** in an article to help you recognize the most important ideas.
- A **timeline** can summarize the important information in a biography.

After Reading the Selection

To informally assess the students' understanding, ask them to summarize each section of Jim Abbott's biography. Use their responses to complete the summary chart on the board or on Graphic Organizer 9. (You may wish to remove the chart before students complete the Focus Skill activity.)

MEETING INDIVIDUAL NEEDS/ESL

To reinforce the comprehension skill *summarizing*, write sentences on the board that summarize several different paragraphs in the biography. Then read aloud the paragraphs and have students identify the sentences on the board that best summarize them.

SUMMARIZING

Comprehension Check, page 74

1. **(Recalling Details)** Ask students to explain what a no-hitter is and to recall the highlights of Jim Abbott's career. D
2. **(Sequencing)** Have students review the events in Jim Abbott's life before he became a major-league baseball player. F
3. **(Drawing Conclusions)** Have students tell about the relationship between Jim Abbott and his father. D
4. **(Recognizing Author's Point of View)** Have students tell how the author of the article describes Jim Abbott. E
5. **(Higher Level Thinking/Inferential)** Possible response: You can tell that he was determined and ambitious because he kept practicing and making it harder for himself to catch the ball.
6. **(Higher Level Thinking/Inferential)** Possible responses: Abbott retired after a disappointing season in 1996; In 1998, Abbott spent a season in the minor leagues.

 Vocabulary Builder, page 75

Have students review the meaning of each vocabulary word. Then have them complete page 75 independently.

Answers for Vocabulary Builder: 1. having a physical problem **2.** way of doing something **3.** non-professional **4.** steadily **5.** surprised **6.** not giving up **7.** did extremely well **8.** round of applause
Extend Your Vocabulary: 9. pinnacle **10.** bunt

Summarize, page 76
Ask a volunteer to read aloud the information in the instructional box. Remind students of the summary chart they used earlier. Then have them complete the page on their own, reviewing the biography as needed.

JIM ABBOTT
GREAT ATHLETE, GREAT MAN

MOST IMPORTANT IDEA OF PAGE 70	MOST IMPORTANT IDEA OF PAGE 71
The story of how Jim Abbott overcame problems can help you see how to achieve your dreams.	Although Jim Abbott was born with only one hand, he learned how to play baseball as a child. He became a successful high school player.

MOST IMPORTANT IDEA OF PAGE 72	MOST IMPORTANT IDEA OF PAGE 73
Before becoming a professional, Jim was a successful college player. He also played in the Pan-American Games and the Olympics.	Although Jim Abbott's major-league career was short, he had great success as a player and continues to be a role model.

1. Jim Abbott is a brave and determined man. He didn't let his disability stop him from becoming a major-league baseball player.
2. Answers will vary, but they should reflect accomplishments mentioned in the article.

 Your Turn to Write, page 77
Explain to students that a summary chart will help them write their own summary about someone whose achievements they admire. Remind them to include four achievements from different times during that person's life in the order they happened.

SCORING RUBRIC

Biographical Summary
Distribute copies of the Writing Rubric Master on page 58 to students before they write.

 4 The summary is written about someone whom the student admires. It includes four achievements or events in the person's life in the order they happened. There are no errors in grammar, usage, and mechanics.

 3 The summary is written about a person's life. It includes two or three achievements or events in the person's life in the order they happened. There are a few errors in grammar, usage, and mechanics.

 2 The summary is written about a person's life. It includes only one or two achievements or events in the person's life, but not necessarily in the order they happened. There are several errors in grammar, usage, and mechanics.

 1 The writing may be about a person, but it does not summarize the achievements or events in that person's life. It is disorganized. There are numerous errors in grammar, usage, and mechanics.

LESSON 10 — WAVES OF TERROR

Student Book pages 78–85

SELECTION AT A GLANCE

SYNOPSIS
Tsunamis are enormous, powerful ocean waves. This article explains what causes tsunamis, the tragic effects of past tsunamis, and the efforts of scientists to better understand them.

GENRE: Nonfiction (Science Article)
Remind students that a nonfiction article gives factual information about a particular topic. Some science articles describe causes and effects of things that happen in nature.

COMPREHENSION FOCUS SKILL

Identifying Cause and Effect

STANDARDS

Reading
- Identify cause and effect
- Use the text's structure or progression of ideas, such as cause and effect or chronology, to locate and recall information

Vocabulary
- Understand the literal meaning of words
- Understand and explain frequently used synonyms

Writing
- Write to explain
- Follow the conventions of punctuation, capitalization, and spelling

Science
- Earth and Space Science: Changes in Earth and sky

ADDITIONAL RESOURCES
Writing Rubric Master, page 59; Graphic Organizer 10
www.tsunami.org

RELATED READING
True Survivors, Steck-Vaughn *Power Up! Building Reading Strength* Level 3

Building on Background Knowledge

What Do You Already Know?
Tap into students' prior knowledge by asking a volunteer to read aloud the text under *What Do You Already Know?* on page 78. Then discuss the questions on page 78 and the questions below.

- When do you think you might see especially big waves? Possible response: during a storm or high winds
- If you lived by the ocean and learned that a huge wave might be approaching, what would you do? Why? Possible response: Evacuate the area because huge waves can be dangerous.

VOCABULARY

analyze	complex	crests	disturbances
meteorites		ominous	phenomenon
seismic		troughs	tsunami

Introduce the content vocabulary.

- Write the vocabulary words on the board. Help students generate a definition for each word, and have them look up any unfamiliar words in the glossary beginning on page 106.
- Ask the following questions to prompt discussion and understanding of the vocabulary words.

1. What are some examples of <u>disturbances</u>?
2. What is an example of a <u>phenomenon</u> that could be <u>ominous</u>?
3. How do you <u>analyze</u> a <u>complex</u> problem?
4. What is an example of something with <u>crests</u> and <u>troughs</u>?
5. When might <u>meteorites</u> be considered <u>ominous</u>?
6. Why might you call a <u>tsunami</u> a <u>phenomenon</u>?
7. How are earthquakes related to the word <u>seismic</u>?

IDENTIFYING CAUSE AND EFFECT

Reading the Selection, pages 78-81

⭐ Get Ready to Read

Introduce the comprehension skill *identifying cause and effect*. Tell students that they will read an article about tsunamis, or ocean waves. Ask a volunteer to read the information in the *Get Ready to Read* box. Then use Graphic Organizer 10 or draw a cause-and-effect chart on the board, similar to the one below.

CAUSE	EFFECT
A tsunami hit the coast of Papua, New Guinea in 1998 without warning.	People could not escape and villages were destroyed.

Have students read the first page of the article to find an example of a cause-and-effect relationship. Record their responses in the first row of the chart. Then ask students to set purposes for reading by asking them to find additional cause-and-effect relationships. Explain that they will complete the cause-and-effect chart after they read the article.

PREVIEWING THE TEXT FEATURES

Preview the article with students. Point out one or more features such as the photographs, diagrams, and map. Demonstrate how to use these features to understand and appreciate the article:

- Some photographs show the damage tsunamis have caused in the past.
- The labeled diagrams show what causes a tsunami and what the parts of a wave are called.
- The map shows the site of the 1960 earthquake and where the tsunami hit 22 hours later.
- Boldfaced words show vocabulary words that can be found in the glossary.

COMPREHENDING THE SELECTION

Help students increase their fluency by having them read one-on-one with another student who provides a model of fluent reading, helps with word recognition, and provides feedback. Point out that the *Tips* in the margins help readers identify causes and effects in the article.

⭐ Tips

- As you read, make a mental list of causes and effects.
- As you read each section, ask yourself, "**What happened**? What caused it to happen?" Look for clues in the article to help confirm your ideas.
- Phrases such as "**for these reasons**" tell you that a cause-and-effect relationship is being described.

After Reading the Selection

ASSESS To informally assess students' understanding, ask them to tell the causes or effects of tsunamis described in the article. Use their responses to fill in the cause-and-effect chart on the board or on Graphic Organizer 10. (You may wish to remove the chart before students complete the Focus Skill activity.)

MEETING INDIVIDUAL NEEDS/ESL

Record students' responses to the After Reading the Selection activity on index cards. Place the cards in two piles: one for "causes" and the other for "effects." Have students take turns picking cards and matching the causes and effects.

Comprehension Check, page 82

1. **(Recalling Details)** Ask students to describe what happens when there is a seismic disturbance in the ocean. A tsunami can approach shore at speeds of up to 500 miles per hour.

2. **(Drawing Conclusions)** Have students explain what causes a tsunami. Tsunamis are not caused by tides.

3. **(Identifying Author's Purpose)** Review common author's purposes for writing. To inform the reader about the causes and effects of tsunamis.

4. **(Recalling Details)** Ask students to tell what events can cause a tsunami. Seismic disturbances include earthquakes, volcanoes, landslides, and explosions.

5. **(Higher Level Thinking/Inferential)** Ask students to discuss what computers can do. Computers may be able to predict a tsunami forming even if people cannot see it.

6. **(Higher Level Thinking/Inferential)** Ask students to explain what a crest and a trough are. If the crest had hit first, people might not have walked into the bay and drowned.

 Vocabulary Builder, page 83

Have students review the meanings of the vocabulary words. Then have them complete page 83 independently.

Answers for Vocabulary Builder: 1. C **2.** E **3.** D **4.** E **5.** B **6.** F **Extend Your Vocabulary: 7.** analyze **8.** ominous **9.** complex **10.** disturbances

 **Focus Skill**

Cause and Effect, page 84

Ask a volunteer to read aloud the information in the instructional box. Recall with students the chart they used earlier to record causes and effects. Then have them complete the page independently, referring to the article as needed.

CAUSE	EFFECT
Meteorites fall to Earth, or seismic disturbances occur.	Tsunamis form.
In 1960, an earthquake occurred off the coast of South America.	A tsunami slammed into the coast of Japan 22 hours later.
The trough of a tsunami hit first and emptied the bay.	People walked into the Bay of Lisbon.
A volcano erupted on the island of Krakatau.	Tsunamis formed, killing more than 36,000 people.

1. A tsunami is hard to predict because of many factors, such as wave speed and wind conditions.
2. Answers will vary.

 Your Turn to Write, page 85

Explain to students that a cause-and-effect chart will help them write about a dangerous event. Remind students to include causes, effects, and clue words that signal them.

SCORING RUBRIC

Article About a Dangerous Event
Distribute copies of the Writing Rubric Master on page 59 to students before they write.

 The article is about a dangerous event. It describes at least one cause that explains why the event happened. It includes three effects of the event and phrases that signal a cause-and-effect relationship. There are no errors in grammar, usage, and mechanics.

 The article is about a dangerous event. It includes a cause that explains why the event happened, but only one or two effects. It may or may not include cause-and-effect clue words. There are a few errors in grammar, usage, and mechanics.

 The article is about a dangerous event, but does not describe the cause. It includes only one effect. It does not include any cause-and-effect clue words. There are several errors in grammar, usage, and mechanics.

 The article may not be about a dangerous event. It does not include causes or related effects. There are numerous errors in grammar, usage, and mechanics.

SELECTION AT A GLANCE

SYNOPSIS
A television reporter gets his big break when his station sends him to California to investigate recent Bigfoot sightings. Does Bigfoot really exist? The reporter is determined to find out.

GENRE: Fiction (Narrative Story)
Explain to students that in narrative stories, the author tells about something that happened. It can be told in first person or third person.

COMPREHENSION FOCUS SKILL
Making Judgments

STANDARDS
Reading
- Offer observations, make connections, react, speculate, interpret, and raise questions in response to texts
- Draw inferences such as conclusions or generalizations and support them with text evidence and experience

Vocabulary
- Use context to assign meaning to unknown words
- Extend awareness of analogies and idiomatic language previously learned

Writing
- Use information and ideas from other subject areas and personal experiences to form and express opinions and judgments

ADDITIONAL RESOURCES
Writing Rubric Master, page 60; Graphic Organizer 11
www.bfro.net/

RELATED READING
From Zeus to Aliens, Steck-Vaughn *Power Up! Building Reading Strength* Level 4

Building on Background Knowledge

? What Do You Already Know?

Tap into students' prior knowledge by asking a volunteer to read aloud the text under *What Do You Already Know?* on page 86. Discuss the questions on page 86 and the questions below.

- Why do you think people have very different opinions about Bigfoot? Possible response: No one can prove whether it really exists.
- Why do you think people are so interested in reading, hearing, or seeing stories about Bigfoot? Possible response: It's exciting to think of what an encounter with Bigfoot might be like.

VOCABULARY

comb consistent controversy developed
eccentric evidence hoax investigate
recovered reverberated

Introduce the content vocabulary.

- Write the vocabulary words on the board. Help students generate a definition for each word, and have them look up any unfamiliar words in the glossary beginning on page 106.
- Write the title *A Bigfoot Sighting* on the board.
- Have students use the vocabulary words to create an interactive group story about a Bigfoot sighting that has occurred somewhere in their state. Record their story on the board.

MAKING JUDGMENTS

Reading the Selection, pages 86-89

Get Ready to Read

Introduce the comprehension skill *making judgments.* Tell students that they will read a story about a reporter who investigates Bigfoot sightings in California. Emphasize that although the story is fictional, it contains clues about whether Bigfoot really exists. Have a volunteer read the information in the *Get Ready to Read* box. Then use Graphic Organizer 11 or draw a judgment chart on the board, similar to the one below.

For	Against
A woman in California said she saw Bigfoot picking berries near her home. Campers said Bigfoot stole food from their campsite.	

My Judgment

Have students read the first page of the story to find clues for the existence of Bigfoot. Record their responses in the box marked *For* on the chart. Then have the students set purposes for reading by having them find additional clues for and against the existence of Bigfoot. Explain that they will use this information to complete the chart after they read the article.

PREVIEWING THE TEXT FEATURES

Preview the article with students. Point out one or more features such as the illustrations, filmstrip, and newspaper clipping. Model how to use these features to understand and appreciate the article:

- The illustrations show who the story's narrator is, as well as events and details from the story.
- The filmstrip and newspaper clipping show information about Bigfoot.
- Boldfaced words show vocabulary words that can be found in the glossary.

COMPREHENDING THE SELECTION

To enhance fluency, have students take turns reading each night's entry with a more fluent partner who can provide a model of fluent reading, help with word recognition, and provide feedback. Point out to students that the *Tips* in the margins help students make judgments about what they read in the story.

Tips

- As you read about the Bigfoot sightings, ask yourself, "**Do these stories make sense? Why or why not?**"
- The main character in this story asks many questions. How would you answer them? Make a judgment about each one based on your **common sense** and what you have read so far.
- Make a judgment about the main character's claim. Is he a good source of information? Is there any **evidence** to support his claim?

After Reading the Selection

 To informally assess students' understanding, ask them to identify story clues that suggest Bigfoot could be real, story clues that suggest Bigfoot is not real, and what their own judgment is. Record their ideas on the judgment chart on the board or on Graphic Organizer 11. (You may wish to remove the chart before students complete the Focus Skill activity.)

MEETING INDIVIDUAL NEEDS/ESL

Write the word *comb* on the board, and explain that *comb* has more than one meaning. Have students read the sentence with *comb* on page 86 of the story and tell how it is used. Have students look up *comb* in the dictionary and discuss the various meanings. Then write the following sentences on the board, and have students give the meaning of *comb* in each one.

1. Do you use a brush or a comb to part your hair?
2. She likes to comb her long hair.
3. A rooster has a comb on top of its head.
4. We will comb the room for the missing keys.

Create a similar activity using the verb *develop.*

Comprehension Check, page 90

1. **(Sequencing)** Ask students to discuss Jerry Crew's discovery in 1958 and the effects of that discovery. C
2. **(Recalling Details)** Ask students to reread the first few paragraphs of the story. E
3. **(Analyzing Characters)** Have students reread the last paragraph of the story. B
4. **(Distinguishing Fact from Opinion)** Have students explain the difference between a fact and an opinion. G
5. **(Higher Level Thinking/Inferential)** The creature was filmed from a distance; some people thought it showed only a man in an ape suit.
6. **(Higher Level Thinking/Inferential)** Possible response: I don't think he'll be able to find the proof, because people have been trying to find proof for years and haven't been able to.

 Vocabulary Builder, page 91

Have students give their own definition for each vocabulary word. Then have them complete page 91 independently.

Answers for Vocabulary Builder: 1. consistent **2.** evidence **3.** developed **4.** reverberated **5.** hoax **6.** controversy
Extend Your Vocabulary: 7. eccentric **8.** recovered **9.** investigate **10.** comb

Make Judgments, page 92
Have a volunteer read aloud the information in the instructional box. Recall with students the judgment chart they worked on earlier to record clues about whether Bigfoot is real or not. Then have them complete the page independently, referring to the story as needed.

MAKING JUDGMENTS

Possible responses:

For	Against
Jerry Crew made a cast of a 16-inch footprint.	The cast could have been faked.
Roger Patterson and Bob Gimlin made a movie that showed Bigfoot.	The creature was far away in the movie.
Many people have reported sightings.	Bigfoot has never been caught.
Recent sightings were all consistent.	Bigfoot's bones have never been found.

My Judgment
Answers will vary.

1. Possible response: I think Bigfoot is real because there have been so many sightings in so many places, the descriptions have been consistent, and footprints have been found.
2. Possible response: I think Bigfoot is a hoax because if it were real, someone would either have captured one or found a body or skeleton.

 Your Turn to Write, page 93
Explain to students that a judgment chart will help them write a short newspaper article explaining their judgment about an unsolved mystery. Remind students to include arguments and evidence that support their judgment.

SCORING RUBRIC

Newspaper Article
Distribute copies of the Writing Rubric Master on page 60 to students before they write.

SCORE 4 The article is about an unsolved mystery that people argue about. It explains the writer's judgment concerning the mystery. It includes three or more examples of evidence and arguments that clearly support the writer's judgment.

SCORE 3 The article is about an unsolved mystery. It states the writer's judgment about the mystery. It includes only two examples of evidence or arguments to help support that judgment.

SCORE 2 The article is about an unsolved mystery and attempts to state the writer's judgment. It includes one argument or an example of evidence in an attempt to support that judgment.

SCORE 1 The article is about an unsolved mystery. It may include the writer's judgment, but there is no evidence or argument to support it.

Student Book pages 94–101

SELECTION AT A GLANCE

SYNOPSIS

This article describes some of the animals that are dangerous to humans. Understanding the habitats and behaviors of these animals is one of the best ways people can protect themselves.

GENRE: Nonfiction (Science Article)

Explain to students that a nonfiction article provides factual information about a topic.

COMPREHENSION FOCUS SKILL

Recognizing Author's Purpose

STANDARDS

Reading

- Identify the purposes of different types of texts such as to inform, influence, express, or entertain
- Describe author's purpose and perspective and how it influences the text and how authors organize information in specific ways

Vocabulary

- Understand the literal meaning of words
- Use word origins to determine the meaning of unknown words

Writing

- Establish a purpose for writing
- Write to inform, persuade, or entertain

Science

- Life Science: Characteristics of organisms; Organisms and environments

ADDITIONAL RESOURCES

Writing Rubric Master, page 61; Graphic Organizer 12
www.bugbog.com/travel_safety/
dangerous_animals/dangerous_animals.html

RELATED READING

Dangerous Animals (Junior Adventure),
Robert Coupe

Building on Background Knowledge

What Do You Already Know?

Tap into students' prior knowledge by asking a volunteer to read aloud the text under *What Do You Already Know?* on page 94. Then discuss the questions on page 94 and the questions below.

- What are some animals in our part of the country that are poisonous to people?
  Answers will vary.
- What would your advice be to someone who is planning to travel to a place where there are animals known to be dangerous to people?
  Possible response: Find out which animals are dangerous, where they live, and what to do in case of an unexpected encounter.
- If you were going to Australia, how would you find out which animals may be dangerous to you? Possible responses: Research online; look up Australia in the encyclopedia.

VOCABULARY

**aggressive antidote fatal hibernate
minimize miniscule native
symptoms treacherous venomous**

Introduce the content vocabulary.

- List the vocabulary words on the board. Help students generate a definition for each word, and have them look up any unfamiliar words in the glossary beginning on page 106.
- Write analogies such as the following on the board. Remind the students that an analogy compares two pairs of words. The second pair must have the same relationship as the first pair of words. Then ask volunteers to give the correct vocabulary words to complete the analogies.

1. Harmless is to non-toxic as deadly is to fatal
2. Generous is to stingy as peaceful is to aggressive
3. Problem is to solution as poison is to antidote
4. Poison is to poisonous as venom is to venomous
5. Tourist is to resident as foreigner is to native

Reading the Selection, pages 94–97

⭐ Get Ready to Read

Introduce the comprehension skill *recognizing author's purpose*. Tell students that they will read an article about the world's most dangerous animals. Ask a volunteer to read the information in the *Get Ready to Read* box. Then use Graphic Organizer 12 or draw an author's purpose chart on the board, similar to the one below.

Author's Purpose	How I Know
to provide information about the world's most dangerous animals	1. _____ _____ 2. _____ _____ 3. _____ _____ 4. _____

Have students read the title and the first page of the article and then identify what they think the author's purpose may be for writing this article. Record their responses in the first box of the author's purpose chart. Then have students set purposes for reading by asking them to find details in the article that help show the author's purpose. Explain that they will use what they find to complete the author's purpose chart after they read the article.

PREVIEWING THE TEXT FEATURES

Preview the article with students. Point out one or more features such as the photographs, subheads, and labels. Model how to use these features to understand and appreciate the article:

- The photographs show the distinguishing features of the animals presented in the article.
- The subheads show what each section is about.
- The labels identify each dangerous animal.
- Boldfaced words show vocabulary words that can be found in the glossary.

COMPREHENDING THE SELECTION

You may wish to promote students' reading fluency by having them reread parts of the article individually. Point out that the *Tips* in the margins of the article will help them identify the author's purpose for writing the article.

⭐ Tips

- The **title** of a passage can give clues about the author's purpose. Ask yourself, "Does this seem like a title for a story or a nonfiction article?"
- An author who wants to inform readers may include **many facts** and **details** in his or her writing. Pay attention to this information as you read.
- Sometimes authors **give tips** on how to do certain things. This can be a clue about the author's purpose for writing the article.

After Reading the Selection

ASSESS To informally assess students' understanding, ask them to explain how they decided what the author's purpose was. Use their responses to complete the author's purpose chart that is on the board or on Graphic Organizer 12. (You may wish to remove the chart before students complete the Focus Skill activity.)

MEETING INDIVIDUAL NEEDS/ESL

Draw a chart on the board, similar to the one below. Help students complete the chart with information they learned from the article. Encourage them to use vocabulary words such as *venomous*, *fatal*, *treacherous*, *hibernate*, *native*, and *aggressive* in the chart.

World's Most Dangerous Animals		
Animal Name	Where It Lives	What Makes It Dangerous

Comprehension Check, page 98

1. **(Recalling Details)** Ask students to reread the third paragraph on page 95. These spiders like to hide in dark places.
2. **(Identifying Cause and Effect)** Have students discuss the snakes that may hibernate when the weather is cool. Diamondback rattlesnakes hibernate inside caves.
3. **(Comparing and Contrasting)** Have students discuss the habitats and behaviors of crocodiles and sharks. Crocodiles can attack on land and in the water. Sharks attack only in the water.
4. **(Summarizing)** Have students refer to the photographs and tell why each animal is dangerous. Animals can bite or poison people.
5. **(Higher Level Thinking/Inferential)** Have students reread the fourth paragraph on page 97. The crocodile would probably run and hide.
6. **(Higher Level Thinking/Inferential)** Have students recall how people react to the animals described in the article. People fear sharks and spiders more than they really need to.

Vocabulary Builder, page 99

Remind students of the analogies they completed before reading the story and have them give their own definition for each vocabulary word. Then have students complete page 99 independently.

Answers for Vocabulary Builder: 1. D **2.** F **3.** A **4.** E **5.** A **6.** G **Extend Your Vocabulary: 7.** *minimus/ minimize*: to make small; **8.** *nat/native*: a person, animal, or plant from a certain place; **9.** *hibernus/ hibernate*: go into a sleeplike state; **10.** *anti/antidote*: something that stops a poison from working

Author's Purpose, page 100

Have the students read the information in the instructional box. Remind them of the chart they used before reading. Have them complete the page on their own, referring to the article as needed.

Possible responses:

Author's Purpose	How I Know
to inform readers about dangerous animals and how to avoid them	1. *The author included many facts about dangerous animals.*
	2. *The title seems like a title for a nonfiction article.*
	3. *The article tells how to avoid dangerous animals.*
	4. *The article tells where dangerous animals live.*

1. The author wanted to inform people of what to look for in case of a snakebite.
2. The author wants the reader to understand that the most dangerous animals are only trying to protect themselves from predators.

 Your Turn to Write, page 101

Explain to students that an author's purpose chart will help them write their own informative, persuasive, or entertaining article about an animal. Remind students to include a purpose for writing and details, facts, or examples that support their purpose.

SCORING RUBRIC

Article About an Animal
Distribute copies of the Writing Rubric Master on page 61 to students before they write.

SCORE 4 The article is about an animal the writer knows about. The purpose for writing the article is clear. The article contains three or more details, facts, or examples to support the author's purpose.

SCORE 3 The article is about an animal. The purpose for writing the article is clear. The article contains two details, facts, or examples to support the author's purpose.

SCORE 2 The article is about an animal. The writer's purpose is not clearly stated. The article contains only one or two details, facts, or examples to support the author's purpose.

SCORE 1 The article is about an animal. The writer's purpose is unclear or contains irrelevant facts, details, or examples.

REVIEW

CLEANING UP MOUNT EVEREST

SYNOPSIS

This article tells about mountain climber Bob Hoffman's efforts to help clean up trash left behind on Mount Everest.

GENRE: Nonfiction (Social Studies Article)

Remind students that a nonfiction article gives factual information about a certain topic. It may also express the author's opinions.

COMPREHENSION FOCUS SKILLS

Distinguishing Fact from Opinion

Identifying Cause and Effect

Summarizing

Recognizing Author's Purpose

Making Judgments

Reviewing the Comprehension Skills

Review the following comprehension skills, which are presented in this article.

- **Distinguishing Fact from Opinion:** Facts are statements that can be proven. Opinions are someone's thoughts or feelings about a subject and cannot be proven.
- **Identifying Cause and Effect:** An effect is what happens. A cause is why something happens.
- **Summarizing:** A summary is a short statement that tells what a story or article is mostly about.
- **Recognizing Author's Purpose:** An author may write an article to inform readers, to entertain them, or to persuade them to do or think something.
- **Making Judgments:** Making judgments means making decisions about something in a story or article. You can use story clues and what you already know to help make judgments as you read.

Reading the Selection, page 102

Get Ready to Read

Help students set purposes for reading by asking volunteers to read the title and describe the photographs. Then have students predict what they will learn about in this article. Ask them to read to see whether their predictions were correct.

After Reading the Selection, page 103

ASSESS Comprehension Check

1. **(Distinguishing Fact from Opinion)** Ask students to identify words that indicate opinions. B
2. **(Distinguishing Fact from Opinion)** Ask students to tell the difference between a fact and an opinion. G
3. **(Identifying Cause and Effect)** Have students reread the third paragraph of the article. C
4. **(Summarizing)** Have students tell what they think the author would most want them to remember from the article. E
5. **(Recognizing Author's Purpose)** The author wrote this article to inform readers about Bob Hoffman's work.
6. **(Summarizing)** The second paragraph explains what makes climbing Mount Everest difficult and why people leave trash there.
7. **(Making Judgments)** I can tell that Bob Hoffman communicated his goals well because other climbers helped take trash off the mountain.

MEETING INDIVIDUAL NEEDS/ESL

To help students better understand cause and effect, write several "causes" from the article on index cards. Causes may include the following:

- Climbers are too tired to carry oxygen tanks down from Mount Everest.
- Bob Hoffman started carrying trash down from the mountain.

Divide the group into pairs, and give each pair one "cause" card. Have each pair list the resulting effect on the back of the card.

Student Book pages 104-105

Sea Turtles in Trouble

SYNOPSIS
This story tells how two children help protect sea turtles in their area by explaining the turtles' habits to a family of tourists.

GENRE: Fiction (Realistic Story)
Remind students that a realistic story includes characters and events that are similar to people and events in real life.

COMPREHENSION FOCUS SKILLS
Identifying Plot
Identifying Cause and Effect
Making Judgments
Summarizing

Reviewing the Comprehension Skills

Review the following comprehension skills, which are presented in this story.

- **Identifying Plot:** The plot is what happens at the beginning, middle, and end of a story. Most plots also include a problem and events that lead to a solution to the problem.
- **Identifying Cause and Effect:** An effect is what happens. A cause is why something happens.
- **Making Judgments:** Making judgments means making decisions about something in a story or article. You can use story clues and what you already know to help make judgments as you read.
- **Summarizing:** A summary is a short statement that tells what a story or an article is mostly about.

Reading the Selection, page 104

Get Ready to Read

Have students set purposes for reading. Ask them to read the title of the story and look at the illustration. Then have volunteers predict what they think the story will be about. Ask students to read to see whether their predictions were correct.

After Reading the Selection, page 105

ASSESS Comprehension Check

1. (**Identifying Plot**) Have students explain why sea turtles are in danger. D
2. (**Identifying Plot**) Ask students to retell the last few events in the story. E
3. (**Identifying Cause and Effect**) Have students reread the first paragraph of the story. C
4. (**Identifying Cause and Effect**) Have students recall what the park ranger explained to Emma and Carlos. E
5. (**Making Judgments**) Possible response: The family steps away from the turtle and thanks Emma and Carlos for warning them.
6. (**Summarizing**) Possible response: The second paragraph tells what Emma and Carlos learned about sea turtles from a park ranger.
7. (**Making Judgments**) Possible response: Yes, I think the tourist family will be considerate of sea turtles in the future because they listened to the children's warning and watched the turtle quietly. They seemed to appreciate learning about the turtles.

MEETING INDIVIDUAL NEEDS/ESL
Have small groups of students write a summary of the story. Remind them that a good summary includes only the most important information from the story. Then have a volunteer from each group read its summary aloud.

Writing a Nonfiction Article About an Activity

Use the checklist below as a guide as you write your article. To get the highest score, be sure you have checked each point.

First write a draft, and then check it against the checklist. Use the checklist to see how to improve your work. Then revise your article as needed.

For a Score of 4

☐ My article is written about an outdoor activity.

☐ My article has a clearly stated main idea.

☐ I have included at least three details that develop and support the main idea.

☐ The paragraphs are well-organized and easy to follow.

☐ The supporting details are presented in logical order with smooth transitions from one idea to the next.

☐ My article has no mistakes in grammar, punctuation, or capitalization.

Name _____

Dinner Disaster!

Writing a Story About a Sticky Situation

Use the checklist below as a guide as you write your story. To get the highest score, be sure you have checked each point.

First write a draft, and then check it against the checklist. Use the checklist to see how to improve your work. Then revise your story as needed.

For a Score of 4

☐ My story is about a sticky situation and is written in first person.

☐ My story includes details that describe the characters.

☐ My story tells what the characters said, did, thought, and felt.

☐ The sentences are organized so that the story events are clear and easy to follow.

☐ My story has no mistakes in grammar, punctuation, or capitalization.

Name _____

Writing an Article About an Activity

Use the checklist below as a guide as you write your article. To get the highest score, be sure you have checked each point.

First write a draft, and then check it against the checklist. Use the checklist to see how to improve your work. Then revise your article as needed.

For a Score of 4

- ☐ My article explains how to do an activity.

- ☐ My article is organized in sequential steps.

- ☐ The sequential steps are all clearly explained.

- ☐ I have included three or more time-order words or other words that provide clues about sequence.

- ☐ My article has no mistakes in grammar, punctuation, or capitalization.

Name _____

Writing a Story About Time Travel

Use the checklist below as a guide as you write your story. To get the highest score, be sure you have checked each point.

First write a draft, and then check it against the checklist. Use the checklist to see how to improve your work. Then revise your story as needed.

For a Score of 4

☐ My story is about traveling back in time.

☐ My story tells where and when I would go and what I would see and do.

☐ I have included three or more clues that help readers make predictions about what happens.

☐ The sentences are organized so that my story is clear and easy to follow.

☐ My story has no mistakes in grammar, punctuation, or capitalization.

Name _____

Writing a Nonfiction Article That Compares and Contrasts

Use the checklist below as a guide as you write your article. To get the highest score, be sure you have checked each point.

First write a draft, and then check it against the checklist. Use the checklist to see how to improve your work. Then revise your article as needed.

For a Score of 4

☐ My article compares and contrasts two animals.

☐ My article explains at least two ways the animals are alike and different.

☐ I have included at least three clue words that signal similarities and differences.

☐ The sentences are organized so that facts and details are clear and easy to follow.

☐ My article has no mistakes in grammar, punctuation, or capitalization.

© Steck-Vaughn Company

Name _____

Writing a Story About a Familiar Trip

Use the checklist below as a guide as you write your story. To get the highest score, be sure you have checked each point.

First write a draft, and then check it against the checklist. Use the checklist to see how to improve your work. Then revise your story as needed.

For a Score of 4

☐ My writing clearly tells about a surprising event that happens on a familiar trip.

☐ I have included at least three details that help readers make one or more inferences about what happens.

☐ The sentences are organized so that the plot is clear and easy to follow.

☐ My description has no mistakes in grammar, punctuation, or capitalization.

Name _____

Writing an Article for a Travel Magazine

Use the checklist below as a guide as you write your article. To get the highest score, be sure you have checked each point.

First write a draft, and then check it against the checklist. Use the checklist to see how to improve your work. Then revise your article as needed.

For a Score of 4

☐ My article tells about a place that I know about.

☐ My article includes more than two facts about the place.

☐ My article includes more than two opinions about the place.

☐ My article has two or more clue words that signal my opinions.

☐ The sentences are organized so that the facts and my opinions are easy to follow.

☐ My article has no mistakes in grammar, punctuation, or capitalization.

Name _____

Writing a Story About Paolo

Use the checklist below as a guide as you write your story. To get the highest score, be sure you have checked each point.

First write a draft, and then check it against the checklist. Use the checklist to see how to improve your work. Then revise your story as needed.

For a Score of 4

☐ My story tells about what happens to Paolo at next year's Carnaval.

☐ My story has a beginning, middle, and end.

☐ My story has a clear problem and a solution.

☐ The events in my story are organized in sequential order.

☐ The sentences are organized so that the plot is clear and easy to follow.

☐ My story has no mistakes in grammar, punctuation, or capitalization.

Name _____

Writing a Biographical Summary

Use the checklist below as a guide as you write your summary. To get the highest score, be sure you have checked each point.

First write a draft, and then check it against the checklist. Use the checklist to see how to improve your work. Then revise your summary as needed.

For a Score of 4

☐ My summary tells about a person I admire.

☐ My summary includes at least four facts about the person's life or achievements.

☐ I have included only the most important ideas.

☐ I tell about the events in the person's life in the order in which they happened.

☐ The sentences are organized so that they are clear and easy to follow.

☐ My summary has no mistakes in grammar, punctuation, or capitalization.

Name _____

Writing an Article About a Dangerous Event

Use the checklist below as a guide as you write your article. To get the highest score, be sure you have checked each point.

First write a draft, and then check it against the checklist. Use the checklist to see how to improve your work. Then revise your article as needed.

For a Score of 4

☐ My article describes a dangerous event.

☐ My article includes at least one cause that explains why the event happened.

☐ My article includes three or more effects of the disaster.

☐ My article uses clue words to tell about causes and effects.

☐ The sentences are organized so that the relationships between causes and effects are clear and easy to follow.

☐ My article has no mistakes in grammar, punctuation, or capitalization.

Name _____

Writing a Newspaper Article

Use the checklist below as a guide as you write your article. To get the highest score, be sure you have checked each point.

First write a draft, and then check it against the checklist. Use the checklist to see how to improve your work. Then revise your article as needed.

For a Score of 4

☐ My newspaper article is about an unsolved mystery.

☐ My article makes a judgment about the mystery.

☐ My article has three or more examples that support my judgment.

☐ The sentences are organized so that my argument is clear and easy to follow.

☐ My article has no mistakes in grammar, punctuation, or capitalization.

Name _____

Writing an Article About an Animal

Use the checklist below as a guide as you write your article. To get the highest score, be sure you have checked each point.

First write a draft, and then check it against the checklist. Use the checklist to see how to improve your work. Then revise your article as needed.

For a Score of 4

☐ My article tells about an animal I know about.

☐ My article clearly states my purpose for writing.

☐ My article includes three or more details that support my purpose for writing.

☐ The sentences are organized so that they are clear and easy to follow.

☐ My article has no mistakes in grammar, punctuation, or capitalization.

© Steck-Vaughn Company

Name _____

Letter to Home

Dear Family of _____,

Your child is reading stories and articles that help with learning to understand what he or she reads. Here are some activities you can do with your child to help at home.

- Get a library card for your child. Make regular trips to your local library and ask your child to pick out a book each time you visit. Discuss the book your child is reading. Ask him or her to tell you about the book and give his or her ideas about it.

- Set aside a time for reading at home. It could be before bed, on a Sunday night, or whenever you and your child like. You may ask your child to read to younger family members.

- Try to read an article from a newspaper or magazine with your child each day. Talk about the main idea of the article. Underline words that your child does not know, and find their meanings in a dictionary.

- Have your child write in a journal. Suggest that he or she start by telling what happens in his or her life each day. You might give your child a notebook to make it special.

Estimada familia de _____,

Su niño/a está leyendo historias y artículos que ayudan a que aprenda a entender lo que él o ella lee. Aquí hay algunas actividades que puede hacer en casa con su niño/a.

- Adquiera una tarjeta de la biblioteca para su niño/a. Haga viajes frecuentes a su biblioteca más cercana y pregúntele a su niño/a que escoja un libro en cada visita. Platiquen del libro que su niño/a está leyendo. Cuando su niño/a haya terminado el libro, pregúntele acerca del libro y que le comente sus ideas sobre él.

- Aparte un tiempo para leer en casa. Puede ser antes de acostarse, en domingo por la noche, o cuando ustedes quieran. Pregúntele a su niño/a que le lea a los miembros de la familia más pequeños.

- Trate de leer con su niño/a todos los días un artículo de algún periódico ó revista . Platiquen sobre la idea principal del artículo. Subraye palabras que su niño/a no conozca y busquen su significado en un diccionario.

- Haga que su niño/a escriba un diario. Sugiera que simplemente escriba lo que pasa en su vida cada día. Podría darle a su niño/a un cuaderno para hacerlo más especial.